Larry the Liberal Lawyer
Lashes Out

Larry the Liberal Lawyer Lashes Out

Larry Atkins

ASJA Press
New York Lincoln Shanghai

Larry the Liberal Lawyer Lashes Out

ASJA Press
an imprint of iUniverse, Inc.

iUniverse books may be ordered through booksellers or by contacting:

iUniverse
2021 Pine Lake Road, Suite 100
Lincoln, NE 68512
www.iuniverse.com
1-800-Authors (1-800-288-4677)

ISBN-13: 978-0-595-36968-3
ISBN-10: 0-595-36968-5

Printed in the United States of America

Contents

Article 1
It's Cool to be liberal...The left is compassion's real home (Philadelphia Inquirer, May 7, 2002).

I am proud to be a liberal.

My heroes are Bill Clinton, Jimmy Carter, and Robert Kennedy. When I see Charlton Heston in a Planet of the Apes rerun, I find myself rooting for the apes.

Here's why I am a liberal: Liberalism means compassion. The real kind: selflessness and caring about others, especially those at the bottom rung of the economic ladder. Liberals fight for women, minorities, the disabled, and those who traditionally haven't had a voice in governing the country. Those are the real American values, if you ask me.

I know: Through the facade of "compassionate conservatism," President Bush is strategically trespassing in this yard. True to his roots, though, he speaks softly but carries a small stick when it comes to helping impoverished people in inner cities.

The Christian Coalition and right-wing fundamentalists claim that God is on their side. Their Bible opposes abortion rights and gays in the military. But another reading sees strong opposition to tax cuts for the rich, as well as strong support for economic policies that show compassion for the poor and oppressed (the Book of Amos), and preserve the environment.

Lately, it's been a tough time for liberals. To stay true to our principles, we should be criticizing President Bush on a number of fronts. That's hard to do when Bush is enjoying record popularity as a wartime president.

But look at all the worrisome things afoot right now: the aforementioned lack of action and compassion; the diminishment in our personal freedoms since Sept. 11; a range of policies, from the environment to social spending, that are simply wrong.

But dissent from President Bush isn't very popular these days. A few days after Sept. 11, I went to a ceremony at City Hall courtyard in Philadelphia. About 50 feet away from me, there was a huge commotion when a man silently held up a sign that said: BUSH STILL STOLE THE ELECTION. People went up to the man and exchanged heated words with him. Eventually, police officers came and convinced the protester to walk away with his tail between his legs.

(It's ironic that some consider liberals unpatriotic because they criticize President Bush—when Republicans made political hay for eight years criticizing President Clinton).

Plus, a quarter century of demagoguery has made liberalism a dirty word. When is the last time you heard a public official or candidate for office admit that he or she was a liberal? L has become the new scarlet letter. If a politician is classified as a tax-and-spend liberal, he or she might as well be wearing an "I luv Osama" T-shirt.

It seems fashionable now to blame everything on former President Clinton: "His economic policies caused the recession! His lax attitude toward terrorism led to Sept. 11." What's next—blaming him for the collapse of the 1964 Phillies?

Let's not forget that Republicans were the party of Teapot Dome, McCarthyism, Watergate, Iran-Contra, Enron, and opposition to the civil-rights movement. Democrats represent FDR getting the country on track after the Depression and winning World War II, the idealism of Kennedy and LBJ, and the Clinton boom. (The Reagan prosperity of the 1980s was misleading because it didn't trickle down to enough people and resulted in enormous deficits.)

Yet I see some friends and acquaintances starting to become more conservative—Bush Democrats, so to speak. It's starting to get like Invasion of the Body Snatchers.

I suppose I should give several benefits of several doubts here. As they age and become more invested in the status quo, many people become more conservative. And after Sept. 11 th, it's been tough to view things from a political perspective. After all, we're Americans first.

So what can liberals like me do during times like these? While we should be patriotic and support the fight against terrorism, we also should ensure that President Bush and the congressional Republicans don't construe his wartime popularity as a mandate to implement a far-right-wing radical agenda.

I'm looking for this cycle to pass, the American memory to clear, and real American values to become popular again. Until then, to my "Bush Democrat" friends, I say: "Don't go to the Dark Side. Stay with us in the blue states."

Article 2
Don't Touch That Dial (Finally, Liberal Radio)
(Philadelphia Inquirer, October 3, 2003 and Seattle
Post-Intelligencer, April 2, 2004)

Finally. The liberal media will soon become a reality.

Last November, an investors' group headed by Mark Walsh, a former technology adviser to the Democratic National Committee, purchased the proposed liberal radio network formed by venture capitalists Sheldon and Anita Drobny. Last month, it was announced that comedian, author, and social commentator Al Franken will be on the new network going head-to-head against Rush Limbaugh in the afternoon. The new network expects to start broadcasting in March or April in New York, Chicago, Philadelphia, San Francisco, Los Angeles, and Boston. Walsh recently announced that the new network reached its first major distribution agreement with the Chicago AM station WNTD.

It's about time that liberals get to be heard.

Last year, the National Association of Broadcasters held its annual radio convention in Philadelphia. Rush Limbaugh, the big, fat, ultraconservative idiot delivered the convention's keynote address—unfortunately his appearance was an accurate reflection of the sad reality that conservatives dominate talk radio.

For years, the conservatives' mantra has been that the media is controlled by the liberal elite. They cite studies that indicate that the majority of reporters indicate that they consider themselves to be liberal. However, the conservatives ignore the fact that media outlets are controlled by major corporations, which tend to be conservative and Republican. Furthermore, even assuming that most reporters are liberal, most of the people who spin the news in this country—columnists, pundits, and opinion makers—are conservative. For every liberal commentator like Molly Ivins, there are at least four conservative columnists such as Ann Coulter, Linda Chavez, Jonah Goldberg, and Cal Thomas. When is the last time you heard Dan Rather, Tim Russert, or Peter Jennings (frequent targets of conservatives) launch into a partisan angry diatribe against the Bush administration?

In the past, liberal radio hosts have failed. The problem is that they weren't angry or entertaining enough. The new liberal radio network can't survive if it serves up tofu and snow peas—it needs to provide red meat to expose the failures and arrogance of Incurious George and his failed administration. There's plenty of untapped anger on the left that needs to vent. Liberal callers are not going to get a fair hearing on the Rush Limbaugh show regarding the unconscionable tax cuts for the wealthiest Americans and the incompetence of the Bush administration in planning for the post-war situation in Iraq. There are also plenty of potential left wing hosts who have the gumption to take on the radical right in an aggressive, entertaining, and sarcastic manner such as Michael Moore, Al Franken, Janeane Garofalo, Paul Begala, and James Carville.

During the months leading up to the United States' invasion of Iraq, most major media outlets served as linguini-spined cheerleaders for the Bush administration. The media did not cover the burgeoning war protest movement until it was too late. It did not raise questions as to what turned out to be darn bad intelligence regarding the existence of weapons of mass destruction and of Al-Qaeda ties to Saddam Hussein. Liberals need a place to vent about the tyranny of King George II without being called dopes, morons, traitors, feminazis, evildoers, and communists. We need a place where the talk show host feels our pain.

Conservative talk radio is simply unfair and unbalanced. It spent eight years lampooning and ridiculing President Clinton through vicious personal attacks. One of the reasons that Republicans gained a majority in the House and Senate and that George Bush defeated (sort of) Al Gore in the 2000 election was the fact that right wing Republicans were getting their message out through talk radio and were able to brainwash enough people to follow them. Hopefully, with the help of a liberal talk radio network, we can send The Cowboy to ride off in the sunset back to his Crawford, Texas ranch.

Here in Philadelphia, there is only one major talk radio station, the big talker, WPHT 1210 AM. Unfortunately, all the hosts are conservative Republicans (one host, Glenn Beck, calls himself Libertarian, but he tends to lean conservative most of the time). The lineup of hosts—Michael Smerconish, Rush Limbaugh, Sean Hannity, Dom Giordano, and Bill O'Reilly sounds like a Bush cabinet meeting or National Rifle Association convention. While these hosts are talented and good at what they do, they only provide one viewpoint—a right-wing, conservative, Republican one. Sometimes, it's like listening to Tass.

You would think and hope that a major city like Philadelphia, which primarily votes Democratic, could have at least a couple of liberal radio talk show hosts.

After years of being abused and ignored, it's about time that liberal Democrats have a forum to fight back. A liberal radio network can help tap into the anger against President Bush and help to ensure that he won't be around for four more years to make things even worse.

Article 3
For the Party's Good, Democrats Must Stay True Blue to Principle (Newark Star-Ledger, Philadelphia Daily News, November 4, 2004)

FOR STAUNCH Democrats like me, it's mourning in America. There was an unusual silence and glazed, depressed looks on my commuter train in Philadelphia on Wednesday morning. Tens of thousands of us had turned out last week to see John Kerry campaign with former President Clinton. Our Election Day hopes had been bolstered by the early exit poll results that were favorable to Kerry, but like other blue-staters, we're now feeling really blue.

Forget healing. Forget unity. Forget "Can we all just get along?" If Republicans want Democrats to join hands and sing "Kumbaya," it's not going to happen.

There are those who'll say that the election results should be a clarion call to the Democratic Party to move to the right and become substantially more conservative. They'll say that it's the only way to recapture the redneck/hillbilly vote in the South and rural areas.

I say: Mend it, don't end it. Tweak it, don't break it.

What's the point of having a Democratic Party that doesn't stand for anything, that abandons its basic principles and becomes Republican Lite? If Democrats become milquetoast, like they did in the months leading up to the Iraq war, there will be no checks and balances on a Bush administration poised to impose a radical conservative agenda on an unsuspecting public.

The Democratic Party has to stay true to its core values—preserve Social Security, fight for the poor and middle class, fight for better health care, work to preserve the environment, and advocate for minority rights.

Over the next four years, we can't overthrow the government, but we need to speak out against the government when it pursues a radical agenda.

Surprisingly, moral issues were cited as the most important factor in the campaign, even more important than terrorism and the economy. In the next few years, Democrats have to convince Southerners and rural residents that they have more in common with them than they realize, especially when it comes to national-security and economic issues. Unfortunately, President Bush and the far right will treat the election results as a mandate. They'll point to the fact that Bush broke the record for the popular vote and that Republicans extended their lead in the House and Senate. But in two straight presidential elections, the results would have been different if Democrats could have picked up only one more state: Florida in 2000, Ohio in 2004.

Congressional Democrats need to show backbone and resist a far-right agenda. They should resist and oppose Supreme Court nominees who are ideologues, not interpreters of the Constitution who respect judicial precedent.

In 2008, there will be a level playing field. The Republicans won't have an incumbent president, and, like the Democrats, there's likely to be an internal struggle as to where the party is headed. Many hardcore conservatives might consider Rudy Giuliani or John McCain to be too moderate for their liking.

And maybe Ralph Nader will be history, which would help the Democratic candidate.

For now though, we blue staters have to lick our wounds and try to avoid the right-wing talk radio gloat-fests.

And if it gets any worse, I guess some of us could move to Toronto for four years. At least they have flu shots.

Article 4

Boss & The Gang; Born to Protest (Musicians Tour for John Kerry) (Philadelphia Daily News, August 26, 2004)

ENTERTAINERS know John Kerry was born to run. On Oct. 1, a group of prominent musicians, including Bruce Springsteen & the E Street Band, Pearl Jam, R.E.M., John Mellencamp, the Dixie Chicks, John Fogerty and Dave Matthews will embark on the Vote for Change tour through several swing states to give concerts in support of John Kerry and against President Bush.

No doubt there will be plenty of red meat at the concerts as Fogerty sings about Bush as "The Fortunate Son," R.E.M. urges Bush to lose his religion, Springsteen yearns for the glory days of the Clinton administration and Mellencamp asks why more Americans can't own their own little pink houses. The 28-city tour will include stops in Ohio, North Carolina, Pennsylvania, Missouri, Michigan, Iowa, Florida, Wisconsin and Minnesota.

The Move On political action committee is presenting the tour, and the anticipated $44 million box office will go to America Coming Together, a group dedicated to defeating President Bush. The artists are performing an unselfish act—they will perform without pay, and they are part of the wealthy demographic that benefits from Bush's substantial tax cuts for the wealthiest Americans.

Given the backlash against entertainment and media personalities who have spoken out against the Bush administration, these performers are taking a courageous stand. Many of them risk alienating a substantial portion of their fan base as well as boycotts. Marilyn O'Grady, the Conservative Party candidate for the Senate from New York, launched a TV ad urging people to boycott Springsteen. Ever since Sept. 11, there has been an air of McCarthyism against dissenting celebrities. Slim Fast fired Whoopi Goldberg after complaints about her anatomical ridicule of President Bush during a benefit concert for John Kerry. Linda Ronstadt was kicked out of a casino after audience members revolted when she dedicated a song to filmmaker Michael Moore. Don Henley was booed when he dedicated a song to Ronstadt.

Last year, disc jockeys refused to play the Dixie Chicks after lead singer Natalie Mains said she was ashamed that President Bush came from her home state of Texas. And the Baseball Hall of Fame canceled a celebration of the movie "Bull Durham" due to anti-war comments made by the movie's Tim Robbins.

Media corporations and the government overreacted to the Janet Jackson wardrobe malfunction by attacking free speech. The FCC specifically targeted and reprimanded radio shock jock Howard Stern for his diatribes against President Bush, which resulted in Stern being yanked off six Clear Channel-owned stations. Right after 9/11, Bill Maher's "Politically Incorrect" was canceled after he opined that the terrorists were not cowards. Two newspaper staffers were fired after writing anti-government columns. In the months leading up to the Iraq war and during its initial stages, the media was hesitant to run stories opposing the war for fear of being labeled unpatriotic. Many believe that musicians should shut up and play and that actors should act, not preach.

But musicians who support President Bush, like Ted Nugent, Lee Greenwood, Jessica Simpson, Toby Keith and Kid Rock, are free to do Red State tours. Entertainers, radio talk-show hosts and the media had a field day ridiculing and criticizing President Clinton, yet they weren't accused of being anti-American or unpatriotic.

After a long era of Britney Spears and N'Sync-type frivolity, musicians are again speaking out against injustice. There's a strong tradition of this, such as Woody Guthrie's political and social songs of protest, Vietnam protest songs, the No Nukes concerts and Live Aid. The entertainers on this tour are not just fighting for their own livelihood. They're striking a blow for the creative expression that our country needs.

By expressing their true beliefs, artists are being true to themselves and their fans. This election is too important for them to stay on the sidelines.

For them, a vote for John Kerry is the only way for this country to become the Promised Land again.

Article 5
Turning Up The Heat While Slanted, 'Farenheit 9/ 11' May Spark Discussion (Detroit News, Los Angeles Daily News, June 29, 2004)

SO maybe Michael Moore's controversial documentary, "Fahrenheit 9/11" does preach to the choir. But as a member of the liberal Democratic choir, I hope that Moore's movie can recruit some new members and change the tune of some swing voters. In amassing almost $24 million in its first weekend, "Fahrenheit 9/ 11" has already become the biggest grossing documentary of all time. What's remarkable about the movie's success is that it isn't being widely distributed—thus, block-long lines and sold-out theaters have been the norm.

While skeptics might dismiss the phenomenon of the movie's success as a result of publicity and controversy, there might be something deeper. It's true that many people who are flocking to this movie are staunch Bush-haters who have already formed their opinion of the current administration; however, since the movie shows disturbing images from the Iraq war and poses questions that the mainstream press has shied away from, it might make some people see things in a different light. I saw the movie at a theater in Jenkintown, Pa., a small suburb of Philadelphia. Jenkintown is located in a swing district in a key battleground state. During the movie, people laughed at the portions that portrayed Bush as a buffoon and applauded loudly after the movie. There was stunned, attentive silence during most of the film, especially during the portions where a mother talked about losing her son, who was killed in Iraq.

After the movie, there were several volunteers standing outside the movie theater, registering people to vote. Hopefully, this movie will serve as a rallying point to energize the liberal base against Bush. There's also the chance that it might convince a few independents and swing voters to vote for Kerry.

No doubt, the right-wing attack dogs are out trashing Moore and his film as unpatriotic, left-wing liberal lies and propaganda. The film shows us many images that most Americans haven't seen, such as severely wounded American soldiers with amputated limbs, bloody battle scenes and American soldiers and their families questioning President Bush and the Iraq war.

It also raises legitimate issues about the Bush administration's ties to the Saudi government as well as its decision to invade Iraq, given Bush administration officials' statements before 9–11 that Iraq and Saddam Hussein did not pose a threat to the United States. Moore's film also raises a legitimate issue about the military's aggressive recruitment of underprivileged teenagers, while only one member of Congress has a son or daughter in the military.

What Moore does through his movie is no different than what Rush Limbaugh, Sean Hannity and Charles Krauthammer do on a daily basis—present and spin facts in a partisan manner. Up until recently, President Bush has received a free ride from the media, which served as patriotic flag-wavers after 9–11 and in the months leading up to the Iraq war. Moore's excoriation of Bush is no different from the right-wing media's lampooning of Sen. John Kerry every day.

If the so-called "liberal media" had raised the same issues that Moore's movie raises, would we have launched this war against Iraq, which had no weapons of mass destruction, no clear ties to al-Qaida, and no involvement in the 9–11 attacks? Would we have been silent while the administration conducted a half-hearted effort to get Osama bin Laden and instead diverted resources from Afghanistan to Iraq? Would we be more outspoken and demand that more resources be put into homeland security?

To paraphrase a well-known Bushism shown in the movie—Bush fooled us once, but he won't fool us again.

It's unrealistic to expect "Fahrenheit 9/11" to win too many fans in the red states, but if Moore's movie can convert 537 voters to pull the lever for Kerry, maybe it will make a difference.

Article 6
Why We Dems Need John Kerry (Philadelphia Daily News, December 4, 2003. Revised version was published in the Dallas Morning News)

WHY ISN'T John Kerry getting some love from the Democratic Party? Is it the hair? The dainty way he eats a cheesesteak? The perception that he's aloof and doesn't connect with people? His wife, Teresa Heinz Kerry, who can be a loose cannon?

Whatever it is, I don't get it. I think that if we Democrats want to win in 2004, we had better consider nominating Kerry for president. I believe that the election will come down to one basic premise—"It's national security, stupid." The economy seems to be bouncing back, and Democrats can't rely on it as their primary issue.

I can't understand why Kerry has plummeted from the front-runner for the nomination earlier this year to an also-ran in the polls. He served as a Navy officer in Vietnam and was awarded a Silver Star, Bronze Star, and three Purple Hearts. He has a specific six-point plan for homeland security, and he has vowed to improve health care for military veterans. Kerry was a prosecutor, likes to hunt and is a member of centrist Democratic groups. He has been critical of the reckless Bush foreign policy, and has stated that his economic policies will be similar to those of President Clinton. He's pro-choice, supports affirmative action and promises tax relief for the middle class, not the wealthiest Americans.

Don't get me wrong. I like front-runner Howard Dean and his stances on most issues. I admire his spunk and the fact that he was among the first prominent Democrat to attack the Bush administration's misguided and arrogant policies on Iraq. It's just that I don't think Dean will play in Peoria, or in the South, given his recent blunder on the Confederate flag. While I don't think Dean would be as big a disaster as George McGovern, I'm concerned that he could be a repeat of Bush I vs. Dukakis. Although Dean's stand against the Iraq war was the correct one, Bush is likely to portray Dean's positions as being soft on the war on terror. A recent poll shows that most Americans believe that the war in Iraq was the right idea. While Dean has bragged that he represents the "Democratic wing of the Democratic Party," the problem is that the liberal base isn't big enough to carry a national election. To win swing states, Democrats can't have a candidate who can be portrayed as a linguini-spined liberal.

Dean is vulnerable for his tendency to make impulsive statements, and he has a lack of expertise and experience in national politics. Even though Dean governed as a moderate, Bush will try to paint him as a radical liberal, and the 2004 version of Willie Horton is likely to be "Jim and John" commercials that focus on Dean's support of domestic partnerships for gays.

A Kerry vs. Bush match-up would be the Democrats' best bet. It would be the Purple Heart vs. the Chicken Heart (Bush went AWOL from his National Guard Service for a year during the Vietnam era). Only Kerry (or Wesley Clark) could get away with showing Bush in his flight suit on the deck of the Abraham Lincoln and make him look like Michael Dukakis in a tank. Most of Kerry's positions are in tune with the liberal base, yet his military background would give him credibility on national security issues with independent voters. I think that, like me, most Democrats would support any of the Democrat nominees in an election against President Bush. Shoot, we would even take a ticket of Homer Simpson and Jessica Simpson.

John Kerry may not be lovable, but we Democrats should learn to love him. There's no beating around the Bush without him.

Article 7
In Iraq, All We've Done is Kick Over the Hornet's Nest (Cleveland Plain Dealer, Philadelphia Daily News, April, 2003)

"So now that we're winning the war, do you still oppose it?"

Some acquaintances of mine at my local gym asked me that question last week. At first, it caught me off guard, but I quickly realized that people all over the country will be asking it to those who opposed or protested against the war. While I didn't join the marches against the war, I had strong reservations against it.

So, were the critics wrong? Well, the fact that we're winning the war still hasn't changed my opinion.

The fact that our troops moved through Iraq with lightning speed doesn't prove the propriety of the war. No one could have reasonably expected that the United States, the most powerful nation on earth, would have lost this war. It was the equivalent of Kentucky vs. IUPUI in the NCAA basketball tournament. However, might doesn't always make right.

Granted, many things that protesters were worried about did not occur—Iraq did not fire missiles into Israel, blow up bridges, set the entire country's oil fields on fire, or use chemical weapons, and the war has not escalated into another Vietnam. The vaunted Republican Guard put up as much resistance as the Detroit Lions or the French in World War II.

No weapons of mass destruction have been discovered, and no conclusive Iraqi ties to al-queda or September 11 th were ever established. There was no proven connection between Iraq and the anthrax attacks in the United States. Saddam Hussein had been effectively contained for 12 years, and there was no convincing evidence that Iraq posed a direct and imminent threat to the United States. We failed to organize a unified worldwide coalition to support the war. Most of the rest of the world sees us as an arrogant bully.

We also still don't know the long-term ramifications of this war. As Egyptian President Hosni Mubarak lamented recently, this war could lead to 100 Osama bin Ladens and increased terrorism. Will the Iraqi citizens and the Middle East perceive the new Iraqi government as a puppet regime of the United States, and cause long-term discord? Will other powerful nations such as China, North Korea, Pakistan, India, and Russia use the Bush Doctrine to their advantage and use preemptive strikes against countries that they see as a threat?

Meanwhile, hundreds of innocent Iraqi citizens and over 100 coalition troops have lost their lives. As pointed out by an article in the April 14 th Newsweek, Arab and Muslim television has focused on the innocent victims of the war, and the Muslim world is united in disbelief that this invasion will lead to a more stable and democratic region. As the article notes, Islamists are calling for suicide attacks against the United States. While the United States sees itself as liberators, many in the Arab world see us as colonial imperialists.

Unlike many of the protesters, I don't believe that President Bush had any malicious intent in causing the war. I don't buy the "blood for oil" argument. Obviously, Saddam Hussein is a brutal dictator, and there was a reasonable concern that he could have given chemical weapons to terrorist groups. However, I don't think that it justified invading a foreign country and imposing regime change. There are plenty of other evil dictators and governments around the world that have chemical or nuclear weapons, and we're leaving them alone.

Is it unpatriotic to criticize the President during a war? If the government and our political leaders are doing things wrong or acting inappropriately, the public needs to know about it.

We need a free press, concerned citizens, and members of Congress, to keep the government honest, respectful of citizens' rights, and on its toes while it conducts the war on terrorism and the war on Iraq. We still need to question policies as to the invasion of Iraq and the aftermath, the adequacy of funding for homeland security, and whether mistakes were made during the search for Osama Bin Laden in Afghanistan.

Hopefully, the war in Iraq will not drag on for too much longer. However, the war against terrorism could last years, if not decades. The guys at my gym and 75% of Americans might not like this, but we still need dissent and people to question our government to keep it honest.

Article 8
Downing Street Memos Must Come To Light
(Philadelphia Metro, June 2005)

In light of blunders such as the Dan Rather incident and the Newsweek reporting of Quran abuse, has the mainstream media become gun shy when it comes to criticizing the Bush administration?

While the media focused like a laser beam on "burning" societal issues like the Michael Jackson trial, the runaway bride from Georgia, and the American Idol Karaoke contest, it barely put a dimly lit flashlight on a critical issue—the disclosure of the Downing Street Memos.

Last month, the eight secret Downing Street memos became public. One of the memos, written by Sir Richard Dearlove, then chief of Britain's Secret Intelligence Service, described his visit to Washington before the invasion of Iraq.

"There was a perceptible shift in attitude. Military action was now seen as inevitable. Bush wanted to remove Saddam, through military action, justified by the conjunction of terrorism and WMD. But the intelligence and facts were being fixed around the policy. The NSC [National Security Council] had no patience with the UN route, and no enthusiasm for publishing material on the Iraqi regime's record. There was little discussion in Washington of the aftermath after military action."

In another memo, British Foreign Minister Jack Straw "said the case for war was 'thin' because 'Saddam was not threatening his neighbors and his WMD (weapons of mass destruction) capability was less than that of Libya, North Korea or Iran.'"

Last week, Editor and Publisher magazine reported that a study conducted by "the liberal Web site Media Matters," found that "USA Today, The Wall Street Journal, The New York Times, and the Los Angeles Times" had "remained silent on the memo and its implications."

Last week, House Democrats, led by Congressman John Conyers of Michigan, conducted a public forum on Downing Street.

The White House has dismissed concerns about the Downing Street memos. Many right wing pundits are on the attack against the "moonbats on the loony left" for daring to suggest that the Downing Street memos should be investigated and could lead to impeachment of President Bush.

There should be a commission established to examine the Downing Street memos, as well as other evidence surrounding the Bush administration's decision to invade Iraq. The commission should be similar to the 9/11 Commission—a bipartisan attempt to find out what mistakes were made and how we can avoid such future mistakes in the future.

In retrospect, it seems as though the Bush Administration ignored the real threat and got tough on the wrong country. While Bush acted like John Wayne towards Iraq, he's acted like Wayne Newton towards Iran and North Korea.

It's hard to tell whether the media is afraid of sticking its neck out on the Downing Street Memos for fear of being criticized as partisan or whether they're just guilty of poor news judgment. There's a big difference between making an honest mistake about the existence of WMDs in Iraq and "fixing" the evidence to deceive the American public and the world into war. If the media had acted in such a timid way over 30 years ago, Watergate would have remained a "third-rate burglary," and Richard Nixon would have finished out his second term.

Article 9
Heckling is not Free Speech (Christian Science Monitor, August 29, 2000)

IN the upcoming months, it won't just be presidential-campaign season or football season, it will also be heckling season. Whether it's a Democrat or a Republican giving a speech, it's a sure thing there will be hecklers interrupting the political rallies. At the recent shadow convention in Philadelphia, Sen. John McCain was booed and heckled so frequently that he stopped his speech and threatened to leave the stage. When it comes to politics, I'm pretty liberal on most issues. Whenever I see Charlton Heston in "Planet of the Apes" reruns, I find myself rooting for the apes. But no matter who the speakers at a rally are, I'm tired of hecklers interrupting them. I've seen it too often.

Back in 1984, I went to see Walter Mondale speak in Philadelphia at City Hall. I don't remember too much about what he said during his speech, but I remember vividly that every 10 seconds a pro-life protester in the crowd shouted out at the top of his lungs, "Baby Killer!" I was furious. I had come to see a presidential candidate speak and this guy was spoiling the event.

Four years later, I saw President Reagan speak at the University of Virginia. Even though I disagreed with his trickle-down economic policies, I wanted to see a president speak. The crowd consisted mainly of young Republican/Alex P. Keaton-preppy-types who loved the guy and welcomed him enthusiastically. There was, however, a group of about 25 protesters criticizing Mr. Reagan's emphasis on defense spending and his laissez-faire attitude toward homelessness and AIDS research. They yelled throughout Reagan's speech and frequently interrupted him. Although I agreed with the gist of the protesters' message, I was angry; I wanted to hear what Reagan had to say.

In 1992, I went to see Vice President Gore speak at JFK Plaza in Philadelphia. Before he spoke, there were speeches by Mayor Ed Rendell and senatorial candidate Lynn Yeakel. Throughout their speeches, a small group of people yelled out, "Sign Item 29," a bill pertaining to item pricing at local supermarkets. Then Mr. Gore came to the microphone and started speaking about the economy and education. The protesters kept shouting "Sign Item 29" at each pause. When Gore would yell "What time is it?" they'd yell "It's time to pass Item 29."

I eventually became furious and shouted out: "Give it a rest already. You made your point." A few others also shouted out: "Enough already; shut up." Gore noticed the commotion and said, "Listen. If you have something to say, I'll meet you over there after I'm done and I'll talk to you about your problem." The crowd cheered and the protesters were quiet the rest of the speech.

In 1996, I went to see President Clinton speak at Independence Hall. During the 30 minutes before his speech, a group of pro-life protesters was chanting slogans and holding up signs depicting Mr. Clinton as the "anti-life" candidate. One protester had a megaphone and was castigating him for allegedly murdering the innocent unborn. Most of the crowd appeared to be pro-choice and generally booed in response to the protesters. I was expecting a riot to break out during Clinton's speech. To my surprise and relief, the protesters were silent and merely held up signs while he spoke.

While there is no Emily Post/Miss Manners handbook on heckler etiquette, it's evident hecklers and protesters have a First Amendment right to speak as long as they don't incite a riot or breach the peace. However, balanced against this First Amendment right is an unwritten code of decency under which hecklers and protesters should let a speaker complete a speech without constant interruption or total disruption. It is a simple case of good manners and consideration for other people.

This is especially true in a presidential race, whether the protesters are liberal or conservative, Democratic or Republican. You've got to give the speaker his or her say. Protesters can get their message across in ways that don't disrupt the speaker—protest and shout before and after the speaker speaks, silently hold up signs, hold a counter-demonstration a block away or nearby while the crowd files in and out. I realize that the protesters at the rallies I've attended throughout the years strongly believe in the ideals they're fighting for. They also want the speaker to realize there's a dissenting view. Perhaps the fact that I remember these hecklers means that their protests were effective; still, they've got to realize that this isn't their forum. For those 20 minutes, this is the speaker's forum, and he or she should be permitted to speak.

Would I feel differently if I considered the speaker to be a vile, despicable person such as David Duke or a KKK grand wizard? No. No matter how hateful the message, the messenger has a right to get a message across. The approach I saw at the Clinton rally was encouraging, and I'd like to see more of it. We shouldn't have to resort to shouting down dissenters or to relying on the speaker's ability to rebuke them. While debate is healthy and necessary for a democracy, there are times when it can be delayed. This is one of those times.

Article 10
Florida Courts Must Settle The Problem of Palm Beach County (Bush v. Gore), Cleveland Plain Dealer, November 17, 2000

Sour grapes. Sore losers. Chicago-style dirty politics.

That's what many Republicans and conservative commentators are saying about Vice President Al Gore's decision to support legal challenges to the Florida presidential vote.

From Gore's asking for recounts to his suing for an extended deadline to allow manual recounts of ballots in a few counties, to his support of the Palm Beach voters' lawsuits, public opinion might sway toward wanting Gore to give up. But even if Gore fails to surpass Bush after the overseas ballots are counted and the disputes over the manual recounts are resolved, Gore should not concede until the Palm Beach voters' lawsuit is resolved.

During the impeachment of President Bill Clinton, Republican members of Congress consistently asserted that the impeachment process was not politicized and that they just wanted to follow and respect the rule of law. They decided to go through with the impeachment even though they knew the odds were slim and that the impeachment would distract the president, polarize the nation and cripple the government for a whole year.

The 20,000 or so Palm Beach voters who had their votes invalidated or incorrectly tabulated will have to live with this the rest of their lives; they deserve to have their case heard. Imagine being a Holocaust survivor or an Orthodox Jew realizing that you had accidentally voted for Pat Buchanan, who stated in his book that it was a mistake for the United States to go to war against Hitler in World War II.

While Palm Beach County voters received sample ballots ahead of time in the mail, these sample ballots did not show the holes in the center. It's easy to say that a voter could have asked for help. But, according to the Palm Beach County poll worker manual, voters have five minutes to complete their ballots, unless they are given special permission.

Many voters might be embarrassed to ask for help. Others might feel pressure to hurry, given the five-minute time limit and hundreds of people in line behind them. Many others might not have realized that they could get a new ballot if they thought they made a mistake. Other voters might have thought they were voting the correct way but later found out that their vote incorrectly went to Buchanan or wasn't counted at all.

Even though "butterfly-style" ballots exist in other parts of the country, they had not been used before in Palm Beach County. A supervisor circulated a flyer around 5 p.m., urging poll workers to specifically inform voters not to double-punch their ballots; however, not all Palm Beach precincts received the flyer. "I did not realize that there was a problem, and I did not receive a flyer stating that there was a problem," says Ruth Silin, a poll inspector for Palm Beach County. "These people have voted all their lives, they are not stupid," says Silin. "But they're used to voting a certain way."

These aggrieved Florida voters should be allowed to use their legal recourse and to demonstrate that there was substantial material irregularity in the voting, that the will of the people was thwarted, and that, therefore, the election results should be thrown out in Palm Beach County.

Many Republicans want Gore to act as a statesman—to act with dignity and class and to concede the election so as to spare the country a constitutional crisis.

Will this open up the floodgates and cause similar actions across the country? Perhaps. But a Florida court should decide whether the law was violated and what the appropriate remedy should be.

A 1998 Florida Supreme Court ruling described the test for ordering a new election in Florida. It determined that it would allow a new election if a judge found there was substantial unintentional failure to comply with election rules and a reasonable doubt that the election expressed the will of the voters.

While a Florida court might determine that the Palm Beach ballot violated state standards, the court would still have to fashion a remedy. In the past, judges have been very reluctant to interfere with the political process and they most likely would be reluctant to order a revote in this case.

It might be a legal longshot for the Florida election to be overturned for voter confusion as opposed to fraud. But that should be for a court to decide. Given the tensions across the United States, a court decision can give legitimacy to the process. Traditionally, courts have been the best places to settle federal constitutional crises, ranging from Marbury vs. Madison through United States vs.

Nixon, which involved the lawsuit over the release of President Nixon's Watergate tapes. Florida state court is the best place to settle a dispute over Florida election procedures.

In the past, courts nationwide have ordered new elections as a remedy for violations of voting rights. In this case, the Electoral College does not vote until Dec. 18. A Florida state court could decide to quickly order a new election in Palm Beach County.

Allowing the aggrieved Palm Beach voters to bring a lawsuit is not politicizing or dragging out the election at the expense of democracy. Everyone should respect their right to use the legal process and to have a court apply the rule of law.

Article 11
Nader, do the Country a Favor and Sit This Campaign Year Out (Chicago Tribune, Philadelphia Daily News, 2003)

Ralph Nader has announced that he will make his decision by the end of the year as to whether he will run for president on the Green Party ticket or as an independent. On behalf of most people on the liberal and moderate left, I beg Nader—don't do it.

Nader has told Green Party officials he is interested in running for president, and he is encouraging "draft Nader" movements. In a recent newspaper story, Nader was quoted as saying, "It is quite clear that the Democrats are incapable of defending our country against the Bush marauders. They have been unwilling to go all out to stop the destructive tax cuts for the wealthy. They have been soft on corporate crime. They have gone along in almost every issue except judicial appointments. So what are you to replace Bush with? They won't go after him the way I could."

During the next few months or so, Nader should come back to reality and do what's best for the left and for the rest of the country. He should take the bold step of announcing that he will not run for president on the Green Party ticket and that members of the Green Party should support the Democratic nominee for president, no matter who it turns out to be.

In the last presidential election, Nader claimed that there wasn't any real difference between the Republican and Democratic parties. The last two and a half years clearly have proved Nader wrong. Even a Bush Lite Democratic candidate like Joseph Lieberman or Richard Gephardt would be a huge improvement over President Bush.

While President Bush has stated that he opposes cloning of humans, you can bet that he will appoint three or four judicial clones of Supreme Court Justice Antonin Scalia. Once that happens, Americans can forget about their civil rights and rights of privacy.

The Bush administration has run roughshod over the environment, which is one of Nader's favorite causes. From global warming to drilling in Alaska, Bush and the Environmental Protection Agency have fostered harmful environmental policies. The Agriculture Department has announced plans to allow logging in 58.5 million acres of roadless national forests that previously had been off-limits. Under Bush, unemployment has skyrocketed and more people are underemployed, yet the Republicans steamrolled a huge tax cut that benefited the wealthiest Americans.

Under the Patriot Act and Patriot Act II, the government will be allowed to invade the privacy of Americans by conducting warrantless searches of homes, checking private citizens' computer files, wiretapping phones and checking what books people have bought at bookstores or checked out of the library.

In 2000, Nader received approximately 2.9 million votes, including 97,488 in Florida and 22,188 in New Hampshire, which helped tilt those states from former Vice President Al Gore to Bush. Nader also took away many of the younger voters who would have voted Democratic.

What's the best that Nader could do in 2004? It would take a miracle for him to win one or two states during the election. Even if he improves his vote count from the last election, all he'll be doing is siphoning off more votes from the Democratic presidential candidate. The only way that Bush can be defeated is if the left can pull off a united front.

Please, Ralph, take one for the team and take yourself out of the presidential race. It's the only way we can send The Cowboy back to his Texas ranch. Your cause is just, but you need to stop tilting at windmills and stroking your ego for this upcoming election. Be realistic and ask what you can do for your country. If you think Bush has been a disaster, just wait; you haven't seen anything yet. Imagine four years of an unchecked King George (the II term) with unfettered power, in control of Congress and choosing Supreme Court justices.

Bush is likely to continue to twist the truth during the presidential campaign and waltz to an easy re-election. Don't make it any easier for him. Please sit out this dance.

Article 12
Protesters Coming (Protests at the 2000 GOP Convention), Philadelphia Inquirer, July 26, 1999). Revised versions were published in the Baltimore Sun, Cleveland Plain Dealer, and as a commentary on Morning Edition on National Public Radio

Chicago 1968 equals Philadelphia 2000?

Probably not. But while Philadelphia most likely will not erupt in chaos and anarchy in the streets during the Republican Convention beginning July 31, the city will be awash in protesters.

Organizations promoting a melting pot of social causes ranging from pro-choice, gun control, labor, environmental issues, gay rights, women's groups, supporters of convicted cop-killer Mumia Abu—Jamal, and advocates for the homeless and the poor are likely to descend upon the city.

You might even get a bunch of people who want to express their anger regarding the alleged civil rights violations by Philadelphia police during their arrest of suspected car-jacker Thomas Jones. Will the city be ready for them, or will this be Philadelphia's biggest public relations disaster since the MOVE fiasco in 1985?

Already, a Philadelphia environmental and consumer advocacy group, the Pennsylvania Consumer Action Network, has formed a coalition of numerous organizations that support liberal causes. It plans to hold a major march and rally with 20,000 to 100,000 participants July 30 to spark what it calls a diverse, progressive movement in the region.

The coalition and the Consumer Action Network, which focuses on consumer rights, clean government, environment, labor and free trade, also plan to follow the major rally, which they are calling Unity 2000, with a week of rallies by individual groups.

Two major unions—the United Steelworkers of America and the Pennsylvania AFL-CIO—officially have endorsed the Unity 2000 rally, a move that could help boost participation and financial support for it. In addition, a Philadelphia activist group, the Kensington Welfare Rights Union, intends to build a tent city for 1,000 homeless protesters called "Bushville."

When Philadelphia was awarded the GOP convention, Philadelphia Council-man Angel Ortiz told the Philadelphia Inquirer, "The people from the neighbor-hoods should come down to the Republicans at the convention and let them know that Republican public policies are working against big urban areas and are not positive ways of gaining minority votes." The Philadelphia police department has established a staff to plan security for the convention. The reported plan is to establish a small demonstration zone near the convention at the First Union Cen-ter, and to have groups of protesters apply for 50-minute time slots at designated periods.

Philadelphia Police Commissioner John Timoney has been studying how police responded to the protests and riots that disrupted meetings of the World Trade Organization in Seattle in December.

He is consulting with police in Seattle, has spoken to FBI officials, and has met with Justice Department experts in Washington, D.C., about the protests.

Concerned that concealing identities was a common tactic during the Seattle and Washington, D.C., protests, the Philadelphia City Council recently passed a bill that imposes a $75 fine on masked individuals who have specific intent to intimidate, threaten or commit an unlawful act. While Pennsylvania is a Republi-can state, with a Republican governor, two Republican senators, and a Republi-can state legislature, Philadelphia is one of the most Democratic cities in the country.

Even though Arlen Specter recently won his Senate race in a landslide, he lost convincingly in Philadelphia to his obscure and underfunded opponent, Bill Lloyd. Having the Republicans convene in Philadelphia seems to make as much sense as the Democrats going to Republican strongholds such as Salt Lake City, Utah, or Pocatello, Idaho. To many Philadelphians, the Republicans will be as welcome as Dallas fans at the Vet for an Eagles-Cowboys game.

Inside the convention at Philadelphia's First Union Center, there will be a major right-wing influence, given George W. Bush's victory in the Republican primaries. It's hard to picture a Charlton Heston keynote speech promoting the NRA being received with open arms in our city. There is a lot more for the city to be concerned about than cleaning up the streets, adding streetlights, and having the homeless out of the way during convention week. (If some people could have their way, the city would bus the homeless to New York for a week for a "home-less Woodstock.")

The desired goal is to allow the protesters to be heard while presenting the city in a positive light for the rest of the country to see. Let's hope that the Liberty Bell and Independence Hall serve as the backdrop for the GOP convention, not chaos in the streets.

Article 13
Kerry Campaign Proves He's the One (Philadelphia Metro, October 2004)

W stands for walloped.

The three Presidential debates were eye-openers for those who had doubts about John Kerry's resolve and his ability to become President of the United States. Instead of the wishy-washy flip-flopper that the Bush campaign ads, Fox News, and conservative talk radio has portrayed, Kerry showed himself to be competent, confident, and on top of the issues. While President Bush wasn't as bumbling and hesitant in the second and third debates, Kerry continued to be more intelligent, concise, and on point. A former ice hockey player, Kerry is basking in his 3–0 hat trick victory in the debates.

While Bush came across better as far as style than he did during the first debate, don't forget that the bar was set very low. His answers were still lacking as far as substance. Bush's only answer to a struggling economy is tax cuts that primarily benefit the wealthiest one percent of Americans. He kept emphasizing education as a solution to the problems of unemployment and outsourcing, but that's of little help to a factory worker who just got laid off and has to support three kids right now. It's apparent why Bush tries to keep himself in a bubble and avoids press conferences and tough interviews. While he comes across as likeable to most Americans, he clearly is deficient when asked tough questions.

The more that people get to see of John Kerry, the more they realize that the negative ads against him are based in Fantasyland.

During the first two debates, he forcefully reminded the President that it was Osama bin Laden and al-Qaeda that attacked America on 9/11, not Saddam Hussein. He also showed that he has a better handle on homeland security when it comes to protecting our ports and nuclear facilities and funding police and fire houses as first responders. During the third debate, it was clear that Kerry had a much better handle on the economic problems that face our country and that he has specific solutions to address those problems.

During all three debates, Kerry connected with the audience and did not come across as aloof and cold. On Thursday night, he spoke poignantly about his faith and his relationship with his family. He displayed a sense of humor when he joked about "marrying up." Most importantly, he came across as Presidential.

This was the confident and personable John Kerry that the voters in Iowa and New Hampshire saw during the primaries. It's also the John Kerry that those who have seen him on the campaign trail have admired. Last month, I attended a Kerry campaign rally at the University of Pennsylvania. There was a huge, enthusiastic turnout. Kerry inspired confidence through his style and message. He didn't just throw out campaign slogans; he gave specifics as to homeland security, the Iraq war, and issues affecting young people and college students.

While John Kerry's performance in the debates hasn't clinched the election, it has caused a significant shift in the polls and stemmed the tide of the Bush momentum from the Republican Convention. Right wing pundits were ready to pounce and say "stick a fork in Kerry, he's done." Now, their mantra is that America is electing a leader, not a debater. Clearly, it's a horserace again.

Any logical thinking person watching the debates had to come out of it with a favorable view of Kerry's performance. Kerry's known as a closer. During the Presidential debates, he showed why.

Article 14
Joe Lieberman's Candidacy From a Personal View (Baltimore Sun, August 16, 2000)

Growing up as a Jew, I always knew that I was different.

It started as a 5-year-old when I wondered why I didn't get a visit from Santa Claus. It continued throughout public school, when I and the other Jewish kids had to sing 15 or so Christmas carols and only one token Hanukkah song during the holiday assembly.

It wasn't until I was older that I learned that being Jewish also meant that I might be a target of hate.

As publicity director of the Jewish student organization at La Salle University in Philadelphia, I got a chill when the posters promoting one of our events were marked with swastikas. I got backhanded compliments from Catholic kids that I was "pretty cool for a Jewish kid."

I haven't felt that chill for years. Like many Jews, I've become complacent about how Jews are viewed in society. Pope John Paul II has reached out to Jewish people and has fostered positive relationships between Jews and Catholics. While Jews were openly discriminated against during the early 1900s in admission to colleges and access to jobs, they have assimilated into American society. While only 68 percent of Americans said they would vote for a Jewish president in 1961, that number rose to 92 percent in 1999.

Even though anti-Semitism has fallen nationwide, Jews are still victims of hate. As evidence, recall the shootings at the Jewish Community Center in Los Angeles and the torching of three Sacramento synagogues last year. As pointed out by the Anti-Defamation League of B'nai B'rith, the Ku Klux Klan and other white supremacist groups are using the Internet to recruit new members. According to the Southern Poverty Law Center, a growing number of college professors are endorsing Holocaust denial theories.

In May, I was walking in my neighborhood when I noticed something unusual. There were police cars and TV news vans parked outside Beth Harambam, a small Orthodox synagogue.

As I got closer, I could see extensive damage—the charred roof, the busted windows, the burned chairs and other debris scattered on the lawn in front of the synagogue, a converted house. A police officer told me that the fire occurred overnight and that they suspected arson.

What really struck me was the symbolism of the yellow police divider strip that stretched between the synagogue's front lawn and the sidewalk. To me, it represented the perceived division between Orthodox Jews and the rest of the community—an artificial line drawn by those who choose to hate another ethnic or racial group because they look or act "differently."

Vice President Al Gore's selection of Sen. Joseph I. Lieberman won't end anti-Semitism. Already, Jewish and civil-rights organizations have reported that the Lieberman selection has triggered an unprecedented stream of anti-Semitic messages on the Internet. The head of the Dallas NAACP, Lee Alcorn, sharply criticized Lieberman. Although he resigned within hours after being rebuked by the national NAACP leadership, his remarks may reflect tensions between African-Americans and Jews.

Mr. Lieberman might serve as a lightning rod and rallying point for neo-Nazi groups, who will assert that he only confirms their fear that Jews are taking over America. Ignorant people will continue to deny the Holocaust and defile synagogues and posters promoting Jewish events at schools. Given the possibility of an increase in anti-Semitism, will Jews keep their heads down and go quietly into the closet so they will not be targets of hate crimes?

Another possible drawback to a Jewish candidate: If Mr. Gore loses the election convincingly, it might take 100 years before another Jew appears on a presidential ticket.

But Mr. Gore's selection of Mr. Lieberman can take Jewish assimilation into American society to a higher level.

It's the political equivalent of Jackie Robinson breaking baseball's color barrier in the late 1940s. It gives hope to generations of Jews who have felt different or targeted as Jews. It further validates the contributions that Jewish people have made to America, showing that a Jew doesn't have to give up his or her Jewishness to succeed.

And the selection of Mr. Lieberman not only shatters possibly the last glass ceiling that Jews had to face but tells young Jews that they, too, really can grow up to run for president.

Article 15

Less-Than-Free Speech on College Campuses (Censorship of College Newspapers) (Baltimore Sun, March 27, 2000). A revised version was published in the Cleveland Plain Dealer.

Should college students be treated like high school students when it comes to running a school newspaper? They can if the Illinois Attorney General gets his way in a pending federal case.

Student journalists at Governors State University in Illinois sued the school after the Dean told the newspaper's printer to hold future issues of the paper until a school official had given approval of the student newspaper's contents. In the past, the paper had published articles and editorials critical of the school administration and had investigated potential problems on campus such as grade inflation and abuse of student stipends. The Dean's order was issued despite a school policy that the student newspaper's staff would determine the content and format of their publications without censorship or advance approval.

In the case, Hosty v. Carter, which is pending before the Seventh Circuit federal court of appeals, the state attorney general is asking the court to extend a 1988 United States Supreme Court decision, which limited the First Amendment protection for high school students, to public college student publications.

Attorneys for a coalition of 25 national media organizations, journalism schools, and civil rights groups will be representing the plaintiff students.

In Hazelwood School District v. Kuhlmeier, the United States Supreme Court allowed high schools to enforce reasonable censorship of student publications if there was a compelling educational reason to do so. The Court stated that its decision addressed only the First Amendment protection available to school-sponsored high school publications, and it specifically left open the issue of whether the same standards would apply to college student media.

In the past, federal and state courts have consistently recognized First Amendment protections for students at public colleges and universities, and courts have allowed public college administrators to censor student media only when they can demonstrate that some significant and imminent physical disruption of the campus will result from the publication's content.

Censorship of college publications has not been allowed even when the material was obscene, offensive, libelous, or of poor quality. Courts have ruled that colleges may not suspend a student editor for publishing controversial articles, withdraw funding because of a school newspaper's offensive content or censor the content of a student publication.

Since the First Amendment prevents only the government and its agents from denying a person his or her free speech rights, First Amendment guarantees of free speech and press do not apply to private colleges and universities.

Irrespective of legislative mandates, court rulings or protections of free expression contained in state constitutions, school administrators should honor First Amendment principles and allow a free press on campus. They should trust its students to act responsibly.

College students aren't clones. They come from different areas and backgrounds and come to campus with their own views. Schools should encourage honest, passionate debate among its students.

A school's fear that its campus would erupt in fights and disruptive protests over a controversial article or editorial in the school newspaper is unjustified. In fact, the campus is likely to become a better, more enlightened place.

Even private colleges with a religious or ethnic foundation should recognize the value of a free press. One could assume that many students and faculty at a Catholic university would cringe at editorials in the school newspaper supporting pro-choice or gay rights, and, that an editorial opposing affirmative action would not go over well at a black college.

However, giving a forum to minority voices on campus is healthy, and it also serves to remind the majority on campus that other views do exist in the outside world.

Furthermore, many of these religious and private colleges advertise and maintain communications and journalism departments, and a neutered college newspaper doesn't set a very good example. School newspapers shouldn't be perceived as public relations outlets for the college.

A school newspaper's criticism of the college or its administrators, even if harsh or sarcastic, can lead to positive changes on campus.

Trying to control the viewpoints expressed in the school newspaper to avoid controversy simply will lead to even more controversy. After all, college students aren't paying $25,000 a year to be treated like children.

Article 16
Some Muggles Aren't Impressed (Harry Potter and Censorship) (Cleveland Plain Dealer, June 27, 2003). Revised versions of this article appeared in the Philadelphia Inquirer and Baltimore Sun)

They're trying to muzzle the Muggles.

Throughout the country, parents, school districts, religious groups, and others are trying to censor the best-selling Harry Potter series of children's books by J.K. Rowling due to the books' alleged occult/Satanic theme, witchcraft, wizardry, encouragement of dishonesty, religious viewpoint, anti-family approach, and violence. According to the American Library Association's Office for Intellectual Freedom, the Harry Potter series has topped the list of books most challenged for two years in a row.

The Harry Potter books received 52 challenges in 2000, which constitute a formal, written complaint filed with a library or school about a book's content or appropriateness. Several elementary schools have banned the books and there are efforts to ban the books from public school classrooms in 26 states. A religious group near Pittsburgh staged a book and record burning that included the Potter series due to its references to sorcery.

In 1999, a school superintendent in Zeeland, Michigan banned classroom readings of Harry Potter, required parental permission for older students to check out the books from school libraries, and forbid librarians from ordering future books in the series. Despite complaints about the ban, the school board supported the superintendent's decision. In March 2000, a teacher and a reading tutor organized students, parents, teachers, and other community residents who opposed the ban to form "Muggles for Harry Potter." (In the Potter series, muggles are people without magical powers). Within nine months, 18,000 people nationwide joined the campaign. Through the efforts of the protesters, the Michigan school district lifted all restrictions on the books, except for classroom readings for kindergarten through fifth-graders.

In being challenged so frequently, the Potter series joins a long list of challenged books such as Maya Angelou's "I Know Why the Caged Bird Sings," J.D. Salinger's "The Catcher in the Rye," and John Steinbeck's "Of Mice and Men."

In Board of Educ. V. Pico, the United States Supreme Court held in a 1982 decision that local school boards may not remove books from school library shelves simply because they dislike the ideas contained in those books and seek by their removal to prescribe what shall be orthodox in politics, nationalism, religion, or other matters of opinion. The Pico plurality opinion indicated that removal of books is permissible where the book contained pervasive vulgarity or if the book was educationally unsuitable. The court stated that the First Amendment includes the right to receive ideas.

While the plurality decision in Pico was not binding precedent, it has been relied upon by many subsequent court decisions. In a 1995 Kansas federal district court decision, Case v. Unified School District, the court held that school district officials violated the First Amendment rights of students and a teacher when it removed a book from the district's libraries entitled "Annie on My Mind," which was a novel depicting a fictional homosexual romantic relationship between two teenage girls. The court emphasized that defendants impermissibly removed the book because they disagreed with the ideas expressed in the book and that this factor was the substantial motivation in their removal decision.

Many great books have flaws and could be objected to on many counts such as violence (Oedipus Rex gouging his eyes out, Piggy being stoned to death in Lord of the Flies); racism and ethnic slurs (the use of racial epithets in The Adventures of Huckleberry Finn or the Anti-Semitism involved with Shylock in Shakespeare's Merchant of Venice).

But how far do you take it? Should you prevent kids from reading the Bible because it contains many disturbing stories? Might a pre-teen boy suffer nightmares after reading about Abraham's binding of Issac and preparing him as a sacrifice? Should you deprive children from reading "The Diary of Anne Frank" because the Holocaust is a disturbing subject?

Authors of great works take creative risks and challenge the reader to use his or her imagination. Otherwise, kids' books would be as bland, non-controversial, sugarcoated, and uninspiring as a Bob Saget sitcom or a Teletubbies script. (Oops, bad example—the Purple Teletubby's gay, according to Jerry Falwell).

With all the evil and violence in society, it's natural for parents to want to protect their young children from bad influences-the books they read, the movies and television shows they watch, the music they listen to, and the video games they play.

But, you have to view a book in its entirety. The Potter books do focus on magic and the occult-there are spells, potions, magic wands, painful curses, wizards playing a game of team handball on broomsticks (The World Quidditch Cup), and dark, vivid descriptions of blood and death. However, there are overriding themes of morality, love, bravery, loyalty, and good triumphing over evil. Harry, who suffered loss and loneliness growing up without his parents who were killed by evil sorcerer Lord Voldemort, goes to Hogwarts, a boarding school devoted to magic, and goes through many adventures with his loyal friends. Harry displays courage by risking his life to engage in a dual with Lord Voldemort and escapes to return the body of his deceased friend Cedric to Hogwarts. Muggle kids across the world have identified and related to Harry as he goes through his struggles. Harry's even made it cool to read books and to wear glasses.

The greatest magic of the Potter series doesn't occur at the Hogwarts School of Witchcraft and Wizardry or at the World Quidditch Cup. It occurs when millions of kids around the world put down a video game or Pokemon card and pick up and be spellbound by a 734-page book.

Article 17

A New Resolve To Walk On Mars (Send People Not Robots) (Philadelphia Inquirer, Indianapolis Star, Dallas Morning News, December 1999)

Houston—We have a public relations problem.

Now that the Mars Polar Lander is lost in space, many skeptics will say that our space program should get lost.

NASA and the nation needs a collective pep talk from President Clinton. Clinton idolized President Kennedy and has emulated him in many respects—some good, some bad. He should do so now—he should explain what we're doing in space and set a specific challenge—to send human beings to Mars by 2015.

The space program has lost its magic. The public doesn't thrill at the thought of the Hubbell Telescope, the international space station, and the Cassini probe to Saturn. The only Moonwalker we've had during the past 25 years is Michael Jackson. In September, the Mars Climate Orbiter either crashed into Mars or burned up in the atmosphere due to metric confusion. A manned mission to the Red Planet would stoke the fires that have been dormant for 30 years.

Like most people, I've lost touch with my "inner explorer." I was eight years old when Neil Armstrong took a Giant Leap for Mankind. I don't remember much about 1969. I recall my parents mocking the hippies at Woodstock and making me listen to Bing Crosby albums instead of letting me experience Jimi Hendrix. I'm also pretty sure I watched the Amazing Mets clinch the World Series.

But I remember a lot about that historic week in July 1969. Kickball, arts and crafts, and knock-hockey games came to a halt at summer camp that day, as they wheeled in a big, clunky black and white TV so we could watch the Apollo 11 launch. For one day, it became irrelevant what flavor the bug juice was that day or who hit you in the head during a dodge ball game.

I was at my aunt's house the afternoon Apollo 11 landed. Later that night, my parents woke me up so I could see Neil Armstrong become the first human being to walk on the moon. That night, I vowed to become an astronaut and to be the first human being to walk on Mars.

Well, 30 years later, I'm chained to a desk all day and I do my walking on a gym treadmill. The closest I've gotten to Mars is through a telescope and an Arnold Schwarzenegger movie. We're taking baby steps and not giant leaps in the space program.

"The achievements of Apollo were so bold and our subsequent efforts so timid that the energy of those years seems like a youthful dream," said former astronaut Edwin "Buzz" Aldrin at a recent space tourism conference. "Had we continued even with that moderate investment in space, about 1 percent of our national budget, we'd have walked on Mars 10 years ago, or certainly five years ago."

Instead of the space race to the moon in competition with the Soviet Union, the journey to Mars should be an international endeavor. Our nationalistic pride won't be crushed if we send a multinational crew to Mars and plant the Olympic flag instead of the Stars and Stripes. There are many people who believe that money shouldn't be wasted on the folly of space exploration. They would note the fact that nearly two-thirds of the world's six billion people live below the poverty level. What about spending money on improving schools, helping the homeless, and curing cancer?

A battle is emerging in the United States as to how to spend our $99 billion surplus—bolstering Social Security, prolonging Medicare, expanding domestic spending, or devising tax cuts. It seems as though funding for NASA isn't even in the debate mix. Shouldn't at least 1% of this surplus be targeted towards a manned mission to Mars?

NASA still has an ambitious schedule for unmanned Mars space probes. Mars Pathfinder landed on Mars on July 4, 1997 and sent back photos and data to earth. Mars Global Surveyor is currently scouting out landing sites for the series of landers and rovers that are scheduled to explore Mars over the next decade. Mars Surveyor 2001 will send a sample collecting rover to Mars for a January 2002 landing. Another rover mission is planned for 2003, and a 2005 rover mission will return a Martian soil sample to Earth.

Every generation has its challenges, adventures, and heroes. This generation's challenge should be to send men and women to Mars and return them safely to Earth. We have the technology to do it. All we need is the resolve.

The adventure of exploration comes with inherent risks. How many failures occurred before the Wright brothers were able to fly an airplane? How many lives have been lost by those who have tried to climb Mt. Everest? Who can forget the tragic fire in 1967 that killed the crew of Apollo 1?

Adventurers like Columbus, Charles Lindbergh, and Armstrong, Aldrin, and Collins led us to new places and showed us what we could achieve. A robot can't do the same.

Let's not dwell on this latest nightmare for NASA. Let's remember what it was like to dream, so that we can one day dwell on Mars.

Article 18
Being Forced to Recite the Pledge as an Outsider (One Nation Under God) (Chicago Tribune, October 20, 2003, and the Dallas Morning News)

Growing up Jewish, I always felt like an outsider as a religious minority. As a grade-school student, I couldn't understand why we were forced to sing Christmas carols during school assemblies. I wondered why couldn't we sing Hanukkah songs or spin the dreidel as well.

Thus, despite my belief in God, I empathize with Michael Newdow, the atheist parent of a 9-year-old child in California, who brought a lawsuit challenging the constitutionality of the Pledge of Allegiance due to the phrase "under God."

Last week, the U.S. Supreme Court decided that it will rule on whether recitation of the Pledge of Allegiance in public schools is unconstitutional because of the words "under God" inserted by Congress in 1954. In its March decision regarding an appeal of Newdow's lawsuit, the 9th Circuit Court of Appeals denied requests from the Bush administration and a California school district to reconsider the district court's determination that the pledge was unconstitutional.

As one would expect, there was a public outcry by elected officials in response to the district court's original decision. Also, as one would expect, no elected official had the courage to express empathy toward religious minorities who are uncomfortable when religion is brought into school. No one chose to cite language in the 1st Amendment to the Constitution stating that "Congress shall make no law respecting an establishment of religion."

Even though I am Jewish, I chose to attend La Salle University, a Catholic college in Philadelphia. Even though there were crucifixes in every classroom, that didn't bother me too much. I was a part of a handful of Jewish students who lived on campus—I was also OK with that. La Salle was a good academic school, I made a lot of friends, and I was involved in many school activities.

What bothered me was that in my sophomore year, there was one class in which the students stood up when the teacher entered the room and they said a

Christian prayer and blessed and crossed themselves. I felt very uncomfortable about this the whole semester, but I liked the school and chose not to transfer to another school. I stood up out of respect, but did not say the prayer.

That incident convinced me that religion should be kept out of the classroom in public schools. It was my choice to attend a Catholic college, but at least I had the choice of transferring colleges, if I chose to. Many public school students don't have that choice.

It's insufficient to say that public school students are not compelled to participate in the Pledge of Allegiance and that they can choose not to recite it along with the rest of the class. The 3rd-grade daughter of Michael Newdow has to go to public school and if she chose to abstain from saying the pledge, she would be ostracized as an outsider by her fellow students. Not all atheists or agnostics can afford to send their kids to private school.

What if Arab-Americans became a majority in a neighborhood in Northern Jersey or Michigan and decided to have their schools cite a modified version of the Pledge of Allegiance as one nation under Allah? Imagine how the rest of the community would act. People are OK with introducing elements of religion into schools, such as saying prayers at commencement ceremonies, just as long as it involves a God that they believe in.

It is disingenuous to argue that the words "under God" have nothing to do with religion. Congress inserted those words during the Cold War in response to a campaign by the Knights of Columbus and religious leaders, who wanted to distinguish the United States from "godless communism." When he signed the law, President Dwight D. Eisenhower indicated that millions of schoolchildren would daily proclaim the dedication of this country to the almighty.

I have no problem reciting the Pledge of Allegiance. Most people in this country have no problem reciting it. But we shouldn't be shocked or offended that there are people who are offended by it and for valid reasons. There's nothing unpatriotic about choosing to pledge allegiance to 1st Amendment constitutional principles.

Article 19
Newspapers Must Do a Better Job of Reaching Youth. Quill Magazine (Society of Professional Journalists) May 2005 issue.

If young people can read 870 pages of Harry Potter, why can't they pick up and read a newspaper?

For the past few years, many people and newspaper publishers have lamented that younger people tend not to read newspapers.

As reported by Editor and Publisher, the Audit Bureau of Circulations' March 2005 report, which was released last month, reported that for the six months ending March 2005, daily newspaper circulation fell 1.9% to 47,374,033 for the 814 papers reporting to the Audit Bureau, according to the Newspaper Association of America. Sunday newspapers had a decline of 2.5% to 51,073,104 for the 643 papers that reported.

According to the Columbia Journalism Review, the declines in newspaper readership are greatest among young adults and the younger segment of the baby boom generation. With many papers losing circulation, many wonder where the next generation of newspaper readers will come from.

Most young people tend to get their news from the Internet or television. I teach journalism as an adjunct professor at Arcadia University in Glenside, Pennsylvania, and Temple University in Philadelphia. Each semester, when I go around the room to see where my students get their news, hardly anyone ever mentions daily newspapers. Kids of this generation are more likely to name Comedy Central's Jon Stewart as a primary source of news rather than The New York Times.

In the last few years, some newspapers have made specific attempts to reach out to this younger demographic group. In November 2002, the Chicago Tribune started publishing a special tabloid newspaper geared toward younger readers called RedEye, which has 280,000 daily readers. Newsday has a weekly "New Voices" feature, which encourages college, high school and middle school students to submit op-eds. The Boston Globe just started a teen publication called Boston Teens in Print, or TiP, that is written by teens. Youth-oriented newspapers also have been launched recently in Dallas and Washington, D.C.

In Philadelphia, I had noticed that the two major newspapers, the Philadelphia Inquirer and Philadelphia Daily News, rarely printed op-eds by young writers. Even for issues concerning young people, the op-eds almost always were written by people in their 40s and 50s.

When I started teaching the editorial writing class at Temple for the first time last year, I was somewhat skeptical. I expected the students to write papers that ended every other sentence with "dude" and that their op-eds would have the depth and complexity of a saltine cracker. I really didn't expect them to have anything interesting to say.

I was pleasantly surprised by the quality of writing of most of the students in my class. I was exposed to subjects that I didn't read about too much in the mainstream press, such as the tough job market for graduating students, admissions policies of the university, housing problems for a traditionally commuter school changing to a residential school and voter apathy among college students.

Many of the papers gave fresh insights on current local, national and international issues. For each of my seven writing assignments, I would receive several papers that I felt would be good enough to run in major newspapers. During the semester, six of my students had their op-eds published. My experience last semester convinced me that there are many talented young writers who are like acres of diamonds that should be harvested by newspaper editors.

In March 2004, John Timpane, the Philadelphia Inquirer's commentary page editor, was a guest speaker for my class. One of my students voiced his disappointment that the Inquirer was soliciting letters and commentary about the 50th anniversary of Brown v. Board of Education only from older people who had gone to school during the 1950s.

He asked Timpane why he wasn't soliciting opinions from today's students. An impassioned debate ensued in which three of my students argued about the validity of kids segregating themselves at the school cafeteria lunch tables. In May, the Inquirer printed op-eds on that subject by those three students. A month earlier, the Inquirer had published an op-ed by one of my students on the anniversary of the Columbine shootings.

Last month, the Philadelphia Daily News, whose commentary page editors had also spoke to my class, published two of my Temple students' Op-Eds.

If newspapers want younger people to read their papers, they should reach out to young people to be part of the paper's community discussions. Op-ed editors should actively reach out to college journalism programs and try to develop voices that have the perspective of younger people. They also need to focus more on issues that young people are concerned about.

Why is it so important to engage Generation Next in newspaper reading?

Because they will be the next thinkers, leaders and voters. Also, there is a great deal of difference between the quick information you can get on the Internet and television compared to the in-depth information you can get by reading the newspaper.

If newspapers can address relevant topics and include younger voices, it's possible that young people might reach the conclusion that newspapers aren't just for their parents and grandparents.

Article 20
Ritalin Abuse Rises Among Teens, Adults (Detroit News, August 15, 1997) Cleveland Plain Dealer, Baltimore Sun, Harrisburg Patriot-News)

Ritalin is a godsend for children with attention deficit hyperactivity disorder (ADHD), a neurological impairment that derails concentration.

But it's not just the class troublemaker or fidgety kid who is taking the drug these days. Ritalin is becoming a popular recreational drug among young people. It's time for the schools to get tougher to help prevent the use of Ritalin for pleasure.

Federal officials recently began investigating public schools to address theft, illicit sale, and abuse of ADHD medications. The Drug Enforcement Administration plans to distribute brochures to schools, recommending safety measures to avoid Ritalin abuse.

ADHD afflicts about 6 million children in the United States, or up to 5 percent of those up to age 18, and 2 million children take Ritalin regularly. Prescriptions for Ritalin have increased by as much as 700 percent since 1990. It is a powerful stimulant and has been classified in the same category as cocaine, methadone and methamphetamine. It allows people who are easily distracted or hyperactive to focus their attention and calm down.

Ritalin is generally considered safe when taken properly, with side effects such as nervousness, dizziness and insomnia. But the drug is addictive and can have serious side effects when snorted or injected, including psychotic episodes, strokes, hypothermia, hypertension, or seizures, and can even be fatal.

In 1994, a Virginia teen died after snorting Ritalin on top of beer. Since 1995, there have been about 2,000 emergency-room admissions per year nationwide for drug abuse involving Ritalin.

The drug has emerged on high school and college campuses and playgrounds nationwide—mainly because it's cheap—$2 to $20 a pill and can be crushed and snorted for a modest high. Many college students take it to stay up late to study. It has been nicknamed "Vitamin R," "Smarties" and "Poor Man's Cocaine."

The DEA and the U.N. International Narcotics Control Board have expressed concern about teen abuse of Ritalin as a street drug. A 1999 survey of 6,000 Massachusetts public school students showed that 13 percent of high school students reported they used Ritalin recreationally.

The DEA reports that Ritalin is among the top 10 drugs in pharmaceutical theft and has found growing abuse and illegal trafficking.

A recent study in Wisconsin and Minnesota found that 34 percent of public school students ages 11 to 18 who take ADHD medication reported being approached to sell or trade their drugs.

Part of the solution may come through strict enforcement of how Ritalin is distributed in schools. A recent study in Maine showed that 63 percent of staff members who give out drugs in schools have two hours of training or less. In response, the Maine legislature passed a requirement to ensure that all schools train unlicensed staff to dispense medicine, according to the Associated Press.

Schools should have strict policies regarding how medicine is stored and dispensed in schools, including how the drugs are logged in, stored, and given out. In Kanawha County, W.Va., students are required to give their medicine to the school nurse upon entering the building, and they must come to the office at a designated time so the nurse can observe the student swallowing the pill, according to the Charleston Gazette. If a student is caught showing Ritalin pills to a friend or if it is found in a backpack, the student will be suspended for five days. If the student has three drug policy violations, they are expelled for a year. Similarly, colleges shouldn't ignore Ritalin abuse on campus. They should have seminars warning students about the danger of using Ritalin as a recreational drug, and students found possessing the drug without a prescription on campus should be punished.

Another solution may lie in the initial decision to prescribe Ritalin. Obviously, kids who have ADHD benefit tremendously from taking Ritalin, and the drug has helped many people lead productive lives. But it shouldn't be treated as a panacea.

In our society, it seems that the cure for every illness is another pill. It's an easy trap for doctors, nurses, and teachers to fall into when dealing with kids who have a condition that is often hard to diagnose. However, you shouldn't push pills down people's throats. Using Ritalin isn't like taking aspirin for a headache; it is a long-range proposition that should be accompanied by other means such as behavior modification therapy and psychotherapy.

What is even worse is the growing use of Ritalin 'just for kicks." The trend of today's students popping Ritalin pills like Pez candies to get a buzz is reminiscent of giving people the pleasure drug "soma" in Aldous Huxley's "Brave New World." Save the drug for those who really need it.

Article 21
School Officials Must Balance Safety Concerns and Students' Rights, (Columbine and free speech) (Cleveland Plain Dealer, January 19, 2000). Revised versions were published in the Baltimore Sun and Detroit News.

"Columbine mania" has infected schools throughout the country. School officials, police and parents are looking for signs and symptoms that could indicate whether a troubled teen is likely to become violent. While their concern is justifiable, a number of incidents indicate that we may be heading toward a new wave of McCarthyistic witch hunts in which school officials overreact and students' free speech rights are violated.

Five days after the Columbine tragedy last April, a junior at a Missouri public high school was suspended for 10 days for comments the student made about the shooting while participating in a teens-only chatroom. The student had answered "yes" to the question: "Do you think such a tragedy could happen at your school?" In October, the student sued the school district, alleging that his First Amendment rights were violated, since the speech occurred outside school time, and off school premises in his private home.

Three days after the Columbine incident, a Nordonia High School student wrote a satirical column that suggested students could relieve stress by assassinating the president and blowing up a house. When the school suspended the student for 10 days for writing the column, he sued the school district for violating his free speech rights and sought to have his suspension expunged from his academic record. The lawsuit was settled in November, as the student received $16,500 and had the suspension expunged.

A pending federal lawsuit in Washington state involves a high school senior who sued the school district and school officials for First Amendment violations after they expelled him for writing a poem that gave a first-person account of a fictitious student who killed numerous classmates and then anguished over his acts. At issue in the case is whether the poem was pure political speech and whether school officials could reasonably forecast that the speech would substantially disrupt the educational environment.

Perhaps the most extreme case occurred last year, when a school guidance counselor told an 11th-grader at a Mississippi public high school that the student's Star of David pendant had to be worn on the inside of his shirt because the Star of David could be seen as a gang symbol. Following a suit by the ACLU and public pressure from Jewish and Christian leaders, the Mississippi school board rescinded its policy.

As the U.S. Supreme Court stated in the 1969 seminal case on public school students' First Amendment rights, Tinker v. Des Moines Independent Community School District, public school students do not "shed their constitutional rights to freedom of speech or expression at the schoolhouse gate."

In that case, the Supreme Court held that school district officials violated the First Amendment rights of three public high school students who were suspended for wearing black armbands to protest the Vietnam War. The court determined that school officials could restrict expression if they could reasonably forecast that the expression would create a substantial disruption or material interference with school activities or violate the rights of others.

In subsequent Supreme Court cases dealing with public school students' First Amendment rights, the court determined that school officials could suspend a student who gave a speech containing sexual innuendo at a school assembly and that high school officials could enforce reasonable censorship of student publications if there was a compelling educational reason to do so.

Perhaps the best approach to dealing with these "Columbine threat" situations occurred last year in Brimfield Township. Eight Field High School students and three Field Middle School students discussed their hatred of some students and teachers while on a Gothic Web site. The students were placed on an "emergency removal list" for seven days pending an investigation during which they were not allowed in school. The students eventually were allowed to return to school after an expulsion hearing. They were not suspended; their absences were considered excused. There was no record of suspension on their records, and they were allowed to make up missed work.

School administrators are in a tough spot in these types of cases, and it seems justifiable to say that they should err on the side of safety. But suspensions or expulsions should not be a knee-jerk reaction, and they should be used in conjunction with thorough investigations, psychiatric evaluations, and/or giving the accused student a chance to explain his or her statements in a hearing. If it can be shown that the student's statement constituted protected opinion or a joke or satire, as opposed to an actual threat or substantial disruption, the school should be willing to expunge the suspension from the school records and reinstate the student. Of course, the defense of joking or satire could become commonplace, but school officials can assess the student's candor and credibility during his testimony, and they can carefully examine the statements in their context.

There's a big difference between the angry rants and specific threats made by Eric Harris and Dylan Klebold and an off-hand sarcastic remark or protected opinions about school violence. While it's justified to be concerned, the accused student should at least be given an opportunity to be heard.

Article 22
Blacks and the SAT: Finding a Better Way
(Philadelphia Inquirer, March 10, 1995)

Lost in the protest over Rutgers president Francis Lawrence's inflammatory racial comment is the unfortunate reality that on the average, African Americans do not fare well on the SAT.

It's a dilemma that can't be ignored. Educators and black leaders need to focus on the environmental and social reasons as to why blacks don't do well on this test, how test scores can be improved, and what colleges can do to provide increased opportunities to minorities.

While it sounds paradoxical, de-emphasizing the SAT as a college-admission factor and increasing inner-city minorities' preparedness for both the SAT and a college-level curriculum are not inconsistent goals.

The 1994 College Board report indicates that the 200-point gap between blacks and whites remains-whites average 938 while blacks average 740. Students who come from a family income between $10,000-$20,000-students who are disproportionately minorities-average 812 while students from families making more than $70,000 average over 1,000. The relationship between SAT scores and the level of parental education shows that the higher the education level, the higher the score.

The data on Philadelphia's inner-city schools are tragic. Forty-nine percent of ninth graders are failing and 20 of the city's 34 public high schools had average SAT scores of under 700. Nearly half of the city's school kids are on welfare.

There are, of course, a plethora of sociological factors contributing to low inner-city SAT scores, including school violence, poverty, single-parent families, disruptive students, the absence of parental involvement and of adequate role models.

In a recent Education Digest article on test-driven school reform, Jeannie Oakes indicates that students in minority and low-income schools have limited access to rigorous courses such as algebra and calculus, and are not encouraged to develop inquiry and problem-solving skills, have less access to well-maintained facilities, smaller classes, and equipment and materials, and have less contact with well-qualified teachers.

In her article on performance-based assessment and educational equity in the spring 1994 Harvard Educational Review, Columbia University's Linda Darling-Hammond states, "Many studies have found that students placed in the lowest tracks or in remedial programs-disproportionately low-income and minority students-are most apt to experience instruction geared only to multiple-choice tests, working at a low cognitive level....profoundly disconnected from the skills they need to learn. Rarely are they given the opportunity to talk about what they know...to read real books, to write, or to construct and solve problems in mathematics, science or other subjects."

Nationwide, colleges are beginning to question the concept of standardized tests as a measure of rating potential students. Two selective private colleges in Maine-Bates and Bowdoin-have dropped the SATs as a mandatory admission factor and close to 200 other colleges and universities have made SATs optional. In Pennsylvania, Franklin and Marshall and Susquehanna University have policies in which top high school students may submit two graded, written essays instead of standardized test scores. The University of Minnesota has an admission index in which high school rank is combined with the ACT or SAT. There is a special review for applicants not meeting admission indices that considers minority status, course of study, grade trends, special schools, activities, and talents.

Sure, the SAT is useful to some extent-it identifies a student's strengths and weaknesses and serves as one indicator of how someone will fare in college. It does not, however, measure intelligence, aptitude, creativity, motivation, verbal communication skills, and work ethic. Past studies consistently have shown that high school grades are better predictors than the SAT of how an applicant will do in college. Schools should be encouraged to continue to look at the whole picture-high school grades, class rank, types of courses taken, essays, recommendations from teachers and school officials, leadership record, and on-campus interviews.

Many colleges have moved aggressively to assist disadvantaged minority applicants who, in many cases, have responded well in the college environment. La Salle University has an Academic Discovery Program (ADP), which admits, on average, about 35 economically disadvantaged students annually. These students, primarily minorities, have SAT scores that generally range from 750 to 850-significantly below the average SAT scores for the rest of La Salle's student body. These students receive weekly tutoring, group counseling, and participate in an intensive summer workshop before their freshman year.

While ADP students have a lower graduation rate than the rest of the La Salle student body, it is still better than 50 percent-nearly the same as the graduation rate for all college students nationwide. The program has produced many successful professionals.

As for the inner-city Philadelphia high schools, they should make an effort to place more minorities on college-prep tracks and provide more challenging courses in English, math, science, and problem solving-something that could be accomplished in Philadelphia as more are subdivided into "charters." Students in non-magnet schools should have schedule flexibility and should be encouraged to take advanced placement courses at centralized locations.

City schools should evaluate, aggressively promote and expand the SAT prep courses currently in place and make a bigger effort to provide tutoring and test tips. Foundations and other private organizations could put up money to give inner-city kids full and partial scholarships to take private SAT prep courses, which cost about $600. Sure, this is no substitute for a solid education, but studies have shown that coaching in the form of math, vocabulary and reading comprehension drills can raise SAT scores as much as 125 points. It's simply another way to level the playing field.

Of course, not everyone is cut out for college. But high schools should try to identify and encourage inner-city kids who show potential and are up to the challenge.

This isn't about affirmative action. It's not about quotas. It's about giving the inner-city kids who work hard and show some potential a chance to go to college to better themselves. They have faced huge barriers their entire lives. The SAT shouldn't be used as another one.

Article 23

No Atheists, No Homosexuals, No Merit For The Boy Scouts (Philadelphia Inquirer, November 18, 2002)

Be prepared for a controversy—the Boy Scouts are at it again.

Last week, Darrell Lambert, an atheist teenaged Eagle Scout in Washington state, was expelled by the Boy Scouts due to his failure to declare belief in a supreme being in accordance with Boy Scout policy. Lambert had earned 37 merit badges, worked over 1,000 hours of community service, and helped lead a Boy Scout troop in his hometown.

While the Boy Scouts of America serve a valuable purpose in shaping the lives of young people, its continued policy of discriminating against atheists and homosexuals diminishes the organization's value and reputation. If it wants to continue to receive funding from various businesses and organizations, it needs to change its ways.

On membership applications, Boy Scouts and adult leaders must say that they recognize a higher power, not necessarily religious. Lambert had disclosed his atheism to Scout leaders last year in his Eagle Scout application, but he still received the award. The current dispute arose last month, when Lambert got into an argument with a Scout leader at a Scout training seminar as to whether the Scouts should expel atheists.

As a private organization, the Boy Scouts are permitted to set its own membership criteria and to exclude certain groups from membership. It excludes gays and atheists. In 2000, the United States Supreme Court in Boy Scouts of America v. Dale confirmed that the BSA is a private organization that could prevent homosexuals from being members pursuant to its First Amendment right of expressive association.

In response to the Supreme Court ruling, many cities and towns withdrew public funds from Scout Troops and barred them from using publicly owned spaces for their meetings. Over 300 school districts nationwide, including New

York, Oakland, and San Francisco dropped sponsorships of the Scouts and no longer provided scout advisers and organizational help. In response, Congress passed the "Boy Scouts of America Equal Access Act," which mandated that local school authorities must grant access to the Boy Scouts despite local policies banning discriminatory groups from meeting on school grounds. However, while schools must give the Boy Scouts access, they are not required to sponsor Boy Scout activities.

Many angry Eagle Scouts, both gay and straight, sent their merit badges back to BSA headquarters as a protest to the Supreme Court decision. Teenaged Eagle Scout Steven Cozza founded "Scouting for All," a nonprofit organization that calls upon BSA members to take a stand against the BSA's discrimination. Filmmaker Steven Spielberg resigned from the BSA's advisory board due to the group's discrimination against gays.

Last month, protesters in Savannah, Georgia called for a repeal of the Scouts' anti-gay policy and urged that the Scouts should give up its status as a United Way agency and should not accept United Way funds. Last month, the faculty at Hamilton College in New York passed a motion encouraging the college to stop giving institutional support to the Utica United Way, which funds the local BSA chapter.

It's ironic that many conservative politicians who support the Boy Scouts' discriminatory policies support cutting off funding for the National Endowment of the Arts and other artistic endeavors that offend their sensibilities.

There are 30 million atheists in America. It is estimated that five percent of the population is homosexual. Exclusion of these two groups has denied many kids and teenagers access to scouting programs. It also has led to the loss of many volunteers who would be terrific mentors, role models, and leaders of young people.

This battle will be won throughout the country on a local level. Religious leaders, community leaders, politicians, and the media must have the courage to take an unpopular stand and speak out against the Boy Scouts on this issue. Businesses and organizations that fund BSA, such as the United Way (which has an anti-discrimination policy) should stop contributing funds to the BSA as long it is keeps its current discrimination policies intact. Several United Way chapters across the country have done so already.

If the Boy Scouts had a policy excluding, say, African-Americans, Jews, Muslims, and Hispanics, you could bet that there would be a huge public outcry. Therefore, organizations representing these and other racial, religious, and ethnic minorities should speak out loud and clear against the Boy Scouts.

Meanwhile, another good and moral Scout leader is lost. Darrell Lambert, who has an exemplary record of Scouting and community service, reportedly doesn't smoke, drink alcohol, or take drugs. He has been a quartermaster and three-time senior patrol leader, an assistant Scoutmaster, and a field leader in training as part of the Search and Rescue Program. Wouldn't it be ironic if Lambert were replaced as a scoutmaster by a crack-smoking, Al-Queda supporting, wife-beating member of the Ku Klux Klan? Under the Boy Scout rules, such a person would be allowed to serve as a Boy Scout leader.

The Boy Scouts serve a valuable function in society in teaching today's youth to become productive members of their community. However, the Boy Scouts' continued values of hate, intolerance, and discrimination against gays and atheists doesn't merit a merit badge.

Article 24
Retest Our Elderly Drivers (Philadelphia Inquirer, April 2004)

Despite popular conceptions, all people over age 75 don't drive like Mr. Magoo. However, there is a growing safety concern about elderly drivers, which the American Medical Association has described as a serious public health issue.

States such as Pennsylvania that have not instituted measures to address this problem of elderly drivers should take the lead from other states that have done so. A study released last month by the AAA Foundation for Traffic Safety said that drivers over 65 years old face a sharply increased risk of death or injury when they drive a car. While other states have wrestled with this problem, Florida has come up with the best approach.

Starting on January 1, 2004, Florida law required that drivers 80 years old or older must take and pass vision tests when they renew their drivers' licenses. According to the South Florida Sun Sentinel, Florida has approximately 700,000 drivers 80 and older. Licenses are renewed every six years for those drivers who have no convictions for traffic infractions and crashes. Older drivers can get their eyes tested at a driver's license office or can get their eye doctor to submit a signed form confirming that the driver's vision is adequate. In general, elderly drivers tested must have at least 20/70 vision in both eyes with glasses.

As reported by the Sun-Sentinel, although the Florida AARP opposed the mandatory eye tests for years, it supported the new law because the state legislature established a task force to help keep elderly drivers on the road as long as possible. It also required state agencies to study how to improve transportation for those who fail the vision test and can no longer drive.

In addition to Florida, at least 21 states have tougher restrictions on older drivers, according to the Philadelphia Inquirer. Illinois and New Hampshire require road tests for renewal applicants 75 and older. Utah tests vision in drivers 65 and older, while Oregon starts eye tests at age 50 and Maine starts at 40. Alaska, Arizona, California, and Louisiana forbid mail renewal for drivers 70 and older. In Nevada, drivers over age 70 must include a medical report with their license renewal. Missouri allows people to submit confidential tips that an elderly driver is no longer safe, which can lead to a driving test or physical exam.

Pennsylvania, New Jersey, and Delaware have no special licensing requirements for older drivers. New Jersey law requires drivers to take an eye test every 10 years, but the law has not been enforced, according to the Inquirer.

As reported in the Bradenton (Fla.) Herald, Florida had the highest number of older drivers killed in 2001, followed by Texas, California, and Pennsylvania. 3,164 elderly drivers were killed nationwide in 2001, compared to 2,494 in 1991. The number of older drivers has increased over 30 percent since 1991 due to the aging of baby boomers according to the Lancaster New Era/Intelligencer Journal/Sunday News, and that arguably has resulted in more driving accidents for senior citizens. By 2030, 25 percent of drivers are expected to be 65 and older, as reported by the Pittsburgh Post-Gazette.

Statistics compiled by the National Highway Traffic Safety Administration indicate that older drivers are more likely than other groups to have a fatal accident at an intersection. Last year, an 86-year-old man drove through a crowded farmers' market in California, killing 10 people and injuring dozens more.

Pennsylvania, which has a higher percentage of seniors than any state except Florida, has no special license requirements for older drivers. It has a Mature Driver Reexamination Program in which 1,650 drivers age 45 or older are selected randomly each month at the time of their license renewal to take vision and physical exams. If they do not pass the physical or vision test, their license can be revoked or subject to restrictions such as being allowed to drive only during the daytime. Pennsylvania also mandates that doctors report patients to the state Department of Transportation whom they believe are driving risks due to a medical condition.

Those opposed to imposing restrictions on elderly drivers assert that such measures are arbitrary and that drunk driving and the inexperience of young drivers are greater risks. They also claim that older drivers are more careful and tend to avoid driving at night or in bad weather. However, many elderly drivers suffer from decreases in attention span, vision, and reflexes, and are unable to see well at night.

Taking the keys away from an elderly driver isn't an easy thing to do. Driving keeps elderly people independent and connected to the rest of the world. While Philadelphia has an extensive mass transit and paratransit system, other parts of the state don't have such a system. Like Florida, Pennsylvania should require state agencies to study ways of improving transportation for those who can no longer drive.

While elderly drivers who fail their renewal eye test will be forced to rely on others to drive them to the supermarket, doctor's appointments, and the beauty parlor, the benefits to overall public safety will be worth it. Having seniors take eye exams is less intrusive and more objective than having senior drivers take a driving test or a physical examination.

Requiring vision tests for elderly drivers isn't a perfect solution and it won't get all dangerous drivers off the roads. While it might be unpopular among seniors at first, hopefully they'll come to see that it's a fair approach.

Article 25
RatherGate Misses the Point (Philadelphia Metro, 2004)

While CBS and 60 Minutes II host Dan Rather should be criticized for their decision to rely on forged documents for their segment on George W. Bush's National Guard Service, many people are missing the big picture behind the controversy.

What's been missing in this story is that, regardless of the forged documents, the premise of the CBS report was accurate—that George W. Bush's family had used its influence to get the future President a National Guard assignment and that Mr. Bush later failed to satisfy the requirements of his service. Several major newspapers, including the Boston Globe published their own independent information calling President Bush's National Guard Service into question.

On September 8, 2004, the Boston Globe published an article indicating that the Globe's reexamination of Bush's military records indicated that he fell well short of meeting his military obligation. There was a six-month gap in his Guard service in 1972 and a three-month gap in 1973. The Globe also reported that Bush's attendance at required training drills was so irregular that his superiors could have disciplined him or ordered him to active duty in 1972, 1973, or 1974. He also did not meet his obligation to join a reserve unit in the Boston area when he moved there in 1973. While Bush was in Alabama, he was removed from flight status for failing to take his annual flight physical in 1972, according to the Globe.

After 60 Minutes II broadcast its segment on George W. Bush's National Guard Service, many document experts questioned whether memos reportedly written by Bush's Commander Lt. Col. Jerry Killian, which indicated that he had been pressured to sugarcoat Bush's performance and that Bush ignored an order to take a physical, were forged. Last week, Republican Congressman Christopher Cox of California asked for a Congressional investigation into CBS News' continued use of the documents. On Monday, CBS announced that while it was deliberately misled as to the forged documents, it was wrong to go on the air with a story that it could not substantiate

Right-wing pundits are jumping with glee over the revelations that call the documents into question. Many of them trumpet this occurrence as the beginning of the fall of the "liberal mainstream elite media." They herald the rise of Fox News, talk radio, and the Internet as evidence of the "new media's" credibility.

However, while the "new media" of the Internet and talk radio clearly has a growing niche, the so-called imminent death of the "old media" is premature.

Sure, the mainstream media makes mistakes, some of them major ones like Jayson Blair, Janet Cooke, etc. But citing the Internet as a bastion of credibility is laughable. Do you really want to rely on Joe's "Blog for Freedom" for your news, when Joe is a part-time real estate agent or a substitute first grade teacher working at home in his pajamas, without any training or real experience in journalism? Not much was made of right-wing Internet gossip columnist Matt Drudge's embarrassing blunder six months ago when he erroneously alleged that John Kerry had had a extramarital affair with a former intern.

Reporters are trained on libel and slander and are much more cognizant as to what standards must be met to constitute reliable sources. Unlike most of the "new media," the major media outlets have many more resources and experts to rely on. While their system of checks and balances through editors and proofreaders isn't perfect, their system is a lot more reliable than Internet site operators and bloggers, who lack the resources to double-check facts and question sources. If Internet sites, talk radio, and bloggers were under as much scrutiny as the mainstream media, there would be many more examples of falsehoods and mistakes.

Even assuming the outdated and erroneous assumption that the media is blatantly liberal, at least the mainstream media makes an honest attempt at being fair and balanced. Most major newspapers and television networks have no clear advocacy agenda like Fox News or conservative talk radio.

It's laughable to hear right wing blowards Rush Limbaugh and Sean Hannity on talk radio along with Brit Hume and others on Fox News brag about their credibility and that they're bringing their listeners the facts. When is the last time they ever gave a positive spin in a story involving liberals, Democrats, or John Kerry?

Most of the time, the mainstream media gets the story right. Hopefully, RatherGate won't cause major news outlets to pull back from investigative journalism, which serves a valuable public service. Also, this controversy shouldn't stop the media from asking legitimate questions about Bush's gaps in his National Guard service, just like the Boston Globe has.

The public takes a much bigger risk when it relies on the alternative media and advocacy media for its primary source of news. It might be exciting and entertaining, but in the long run, an informed person would rather rely on CBS and the mainstream media.

Article 26
Icing Tort Reform (Philadelphia Inquirer, July 17, 1998)

Tort reform sounds like a novel way to prepare fancy European pastries. But it's a serious issue that affects all of us.

Last week, Senate Democrats blocked passage of a proposed federal products liability bill negotiated by the White House, Senator Jay Rockefeller, and Senator Slade Gordon. The proposed bill would have set national standards for lawsuits against companies that make harmful products and would have preempted products liability standards in all 50 states.

In addition to providing nationwide products liability standards, the bill would have provided immunity for retailers and wholesalers unless they had altered the product that caused the harm or the manufacturer had gone out of business. It also would have limited punitive damages to be paid by small businesses-companies with fewer than 25 employees or less than $5 million in annual revenue. The punitive damages would have been limited to $250,000 or twice the actual damages, that is, medical expenses and lost wages. It also would have limited punitive damages to cases in which plaintiff consumers could show clear and convincing evidence that they were harmed by a manufacturer's conscious and flagrant indifference to the safety of others.

More than 200 organizations opposed the legislation, including consumer advocates such as Public Citizen, New Jersey and Pennsylvania Public Interest Research Group, and Ralph Nader.

In 1996, President Clinton vetoed a broader tort reform bill, claiming that it "tilted the playing field against consumers." Republicans charged that Clinton caved into the demands of the trial lawyers who contributed heavily to his reelection campaign.

Restricting products liability lawsuits has been a long-time priority for businesses, which argue that a litigation explosion has occurred in which out-of-control juries are awarding excessive punitive damages. They argue that products liability lawsuits lead to skyrocketing litigation costs and liability insurance rates, lost jobs, rising consumer prices, and the closing of organizations such as hospitals, day care centers, ski resorts, and public swimming pools that can't afford such costs. Advocates of tort reform complain about lengthy delays in getting cases to trial, high attorneys' fees, overly generous damage awards, and the possibility that the fear of large damage awards deters businesses from product innovations. They assert that because businesses are targeted by litigation-happy lawyers as rich "deep pockets," they are faced with frivolous cases that they are forced to settle rather than risk huge jury awards.

While tort reform is packaged by its advocates to sound like a progressive philosophy that benefits everyone, in reality, its actual effect of limiting consumer lawsuits would make manufacturers less responsive to complaints about defective goods and deprive many individuals who have been injured by a defective product of an effective remedy. Limiting punitive damages would give manufacturers less exposure for any defects in their products and make it more likely that defective products would remain on the market. Setting arbitrary limits on damages as a general tort reform goal could have the effect of rendering damages inadequate in situations involving brain damage, paralysis, burn injuries, or chronic medical problems.

Contrary to businesses' assertions, punitive damage awards in products liability cases are rare, and those that are made result in positive improvements in the product.

Public Citizen cites academic studies showing that there were only 379 punitive damage awards in state and federal products liability lawsuits between 1965 and 1994-an average of 13 per year. Many of these awards were reduced or overturned on appeal. One study showed that in nearly 80% of those cases the manufacturer took some subsequent safety measure in the wake of punitive damages. The Small Business Administration reported in 1997 that almost 80% of the 327,805 manufacturing companies in the United States are businesses of 25 employees or fewer.

Another concern about the federal legislation is that the federal government is getting involved at all. This issue is best resolved at the state level, where it traditionally has been. Some states have chosen to be more pro-business and have enacted legislation that discourages the filing of products liability suits by placing caps on punitive damages and noneconomic damages, such as pain and suffering, and by shortening statutes of limitations for bringing suit. Other states are more pro-consumer and have no damages cap or allow larger damages than the proposed federal bill.

It might seem fashionable and indeed often appropriate to bash trial lawyers and to put them one step below carjackers and mass murderers. However, without trial lawyers and contingent fee arrangements, most victims of defective products would have little or no access to courts. Furthermore, there are rules that provide sanctions against attorneys who file frivolous lawsuits. By portraying trial lawyers as the "poster children" of tort reform, its advocates deliberately shift the focus away from the victims of defective products. The real victims are drivers of Sport Utility Vehicles that roll over; children who suffer severe burns because of pajamas that are not fire retardant; and homeowners who are injured in a propane gas explosion because the supplier failed properly to odorize the gas.

The current products liability system isn't perfect, but it works fairly well in punishing and preventing corporate neglect and misconduct and in compensating injured consumers. The current proposed federal bill, like most tort reform measures, shifts most of the risk back to the consumer. It's a recipe for concern.

Article 27
Beware of Cable Guys Snooping Around the Neighborhood (Operation TIPS) (Chicago Tribune, July 23, 2002)

Big Brother is about to start watching you. Next month, Operation TIPS (Terrorism Information and Prevention System), a national system administered by the U.S. Department of Justice that is designed to be a central reporting point for suspicious and potentially terrorist-related activity, will begin operating. While the program may be well-intentioned, it could lead to a police state in which our civil rights and privacy will be endangered.

Operation TIPS will involve millions of American workers, such as cable installers, plumbers, meter readers and gas or electrical technicians who, in the course of their work, are in position to spot so-called unusual or suspicious activity in customers' homes and will be called upon to act as volunteer informants. Reported information will go to a central database at the Justice Department. The program will begin in 10 cities and then expand nationwide. According to Operation TIPS' Web site, "These workers will use their common sense and knowledge of their work environment to identify suspicious or unusual activity."

The United States Postal Service announced Wednesday that it would not participate in Operation TIPS. However, the next day, it stated that it had decided to meet with the Justice Department about participating. The Postal Service, along with other agencies and utilities, should have the courage to step forward and refuse to participate in the program.

Many Americans likely will support this program given the scary times that we live in. They won't care if the cable guy becomes a government spy.

However, I'm sure that most Americans would not want their cable installer to be spying on them. Civil-rights groups such as the American Civil Liberties Union have expressed concern that Operation TIPS volunteers would be conducting illegal searches of people's homes without warrants.

Ever since Sept. 11, many if not most of us probably have engaged in racial profiling of Arab-Americans. Earlier this year, I took a train from Florida to Philadelphia. One of the passengers who boarded the train in Florida seemed to me to be suspicious. He appeared to be Arabic, he seemed to be nervous and was making frequent calls on his cell phone and was having animated conversations in a foreign language that I assumed was Arabic. He also had two large carry-on bags that I was worried could contain a bomb.

I thought about telling the conductor about my suspicions, but I decided to wait it out. Later on during the trip, I found out that the "suspicious man" was an Orthodox Jew of Israeli descent who lived five miles from me in Philadelphia and who was a member of my cousins' synagogue.

I jumped to a conclusion about that man based on his appearance, and there will likely be thousands of useless tips and false calls during the course of Operation TIPS because untrained workers are bound to jump to similar erroneous conclusions.

Is someone suspicious because he appears to be of Arab descent? Because he has a Koran or an Arabic newspaper on his living room coffee table? Should your local librarian report you for taking out books on Arab culture? Will your local cable guy want to go from being Jim Carrey to instead be James Bond or Austin Powers in fighting evildoers?

These volunteer workers might become overly vigilant in their desire to become heroes. There also is a danger that they might concoct false information or plant items as part of a vendetta against a customer. For all we know, many of these volunteer informants could have criminal backgrounds of their own.

Obviously, our country needs to crack down on potential terrorists to prevent other disasters. But let's leave it to the experts. The government should enforce existing immigration laws and the FBI and police should continue surveillance activity.

But giving the Maytag repairman something to do is a decision we'll all regret later.

Article 28
Our Youth Embody The Gift of Giving (Youth Volunteerism) (Newsday, February 19, 2002). Revised versions of this Op-Ed were published in the Philadelphia Inquirer, Baltimore Sun, Los Angeles Daily News, Cleveland Plain Dealer)

PRESIDENT George W. Bush's clarion call during his State of the Union speech for Americans to get involved in community and volunteerism was well-intentioned, but it overlooked the fact that the youth of this nation are already several steps ahead of him.

Despite all of the lamenting about the apathy, narcissism, and decline in values and morals of today's young people, there is one sign that contradicts this stereotype. This generation of young people is more active in volunteering and giving than perhaps any generation that came before it. President Bush should have made the gesture of inviting youth volunteers to the State of the Union audience and acknowledging them during his speech.

According to figures from the Points of Light Foundation in Washington, 13 million teenagers—or 59 percent of America's teen population—volunteer more than 3.5 hours a week. A 1998 national survey reported that about one-third of students in grades seven through 12 identified volunteering and helping others as very important goals. According to a national survey of college students conducted by the Institute of Politics at Harvard University, 60 percent of the students said they preferred community volunteerism to political engagement as a better way to solve important issues facing the country.

It's ironic that Bush is attempting to seize the issue of volunteerism and community service from Democrats. One of the hallmarks of Bill Clinton's presidency was the creation of AmeriCorps, and he also presided over the 1997 national Summit for Volunteerism in Philadelphia. Over the past few years, many Republicans have criticized social programs such as AmeriCorps and midnight basketball in inner cities. Last April, 3 million young people nationwide participated in National Youth Service Day by engaging in more than 10,000 community improvement projects in all 50 states. The number of AmeriCorps national service volunteers has grown from 20,000 in 1994 to 40,000 today, and the number of City Year organization affiliates has grown from one city in 1988 to 13 today.

New York-area students are in on the act, too. Long Island University students, for instance, participate in volunteer projects such as beach cleanups, tutoring, and being Big Brothers and Big Sisters. New York University's C-Team consists of more than 250 student volunteers who participate in community service projects such as providing teacher support, tutoring, and creating special classes in such areas as dance, photography, cooking and karate for disadvantaged schools in Manhattan. Students in Bayside's Benjamin N. Cardozo High School Key Club—part of a Kiwanis-sponsored national service organization for high school students—have participated in many volunteer projects during the past few years, including visits to the Ronald McDonald House in Queens and the Long Island Jewish Hospital Geriatric Center, conducting canned food drives for City Harvest and volunteering at the Holy Apostle Soup Kitchen in Manhattan.

Key Club members at East Meadow High School help local elementary school kids with their homework, sell doughnuts to raise money for the Make-a-Wish Foundation and volunteer at Nassau University Medical Center.

Society can't hold it against today's young people that—until lately, at least—there have been no great social issues to get angry and protest about, such as the Vietnam War. Unlike the "Greatest Generation," they haven't had to live through crises such as the Great Depression and World War II. And while the terrorist attack on Sept. 11 has affected everyone in this country emotionally, even it hasn't had a direct impact on the lives of young people outside of New York and Washington.

Although issues such as the environment, child labor abuse in foreign countries and world hunger are very important, they don't have an immediate and mobilizing effect on young people's lives so as to cause mass protests in the streets and on campuses.

Engaging in volunteerism is the way this generation has seen fit to try to make a difference. When they volunteer, they get to see an immediate, positive impact on other people's lives—parks, schools and recreational centers get cleaned up, a young child improves his reading skills, a nursing-home resident gets a new friend and money gets raised for various charities.

While the president's call for people to dedicate 4,000 hours toward community service during their lives may sound like a daunting proposition, it's realistic when you break it down. Over a 40-year period, an individual would have to volunteer 100 hours a year, or two hours a week. But even if many people can't meet the 4,000-hour goal, increased volunteerism is realistic because of the volunteer spirit that already existed in today's young people. Instead of parents dragging kids to Little League, maybe we'll see kids dragging their parents to volunteer for a Special Olympics track meet or at a homeless shelter. The spirit of youth volunteerism also is likely to spread to older people.

There's a lot more to this younger generation than tattoos, nose rings and Limp Bizkit. President Bush and others should give them credit for it.

Article 29
Media attacked for doing their job (Baltimore Sun, Cleveland Plain Dealer, November 6, 2001)

Since Sept. 11, the American media have aired a lot of controversial opinions:

Give peace a chance.

President Bush is mishandling the war.

Let's start deporting Arabs and drop nuclear bombs on Afghanistan.

The United States should stop its unilateral support of Israel.

These might be unpopular opinions to many, but should columnists and journalists be excoriated if they express them in their articles? Free speech by journalists is essential in our society, but in the aftermath of Sept. 11 it has been open season on those in the media who have attempted to assert their free speech rights.

Last month, columnists in Oregon and Texas were fired after they criticized President Bush. According to the Association of Alternative Newspapers, advertisers in many alternative weekly newspapers have either canceled ads or threatened to after the appearance of columns criticizing Mr. Bush. Aaron McGruder, the creator of the comic strip The Boondocks, mocked American patriotism after the Sept. 11 attacks; in response, The Boondocks was pulled from at least three newspapers—New York's Daily News, Newsday and the Dallas Morning News. White House press secretary Ari Fleischer may have been prophetic when he warned Americans that "they need to watch what they say, watch what they do."

Is it unpatriotic to criticize the president during a war? A columnist's job is to offer his or her opinion, and a muzzled or self-censored columnist is as useful as an opera singer with laryngitis. If the government and our political leaders are doing things wrong or acting inappropriately, the public needs to know about it.

Dissent is healthy, not anti-American. In fact, both the urge and the opportunity to disagree with authorities, guaranteed by the First Amendment, represent the most core American values of them all.

If it hadn't been for free speech, media coverage and dissent, the Vietnam War might have dragged on for many more years. The press had great access in covering that war, and the brutality of Vietnam was brought into America's living rooms each night.

Without free speech and the efforts of journalists, the Watergate scandal might never have been exposed.

Yet, with President Bush, everyone, especially those in the media, has been expected to be a team player and to agree with everything our government does.

But it is legitimate for journalists to ask questions and foster vigorous debate about wartime events, now and in the future. They shouldn't be castigated if they choose to raise questions such as whether the federal government's response to the anthrax attacks was adequate since it led to the deaths of two Washington post office workers.

Will Americans still wholeheartedly support the war if our troops get bogged down in a Vietnam-like quagmire in Afghanistan? If the war spreads and more troops are needed, will people be willing to accept a draft?

Some believe that dissenters are unpatriotic and a disgrace to the country. It's terrific that Americans have bonded together after the Sept. 11 attack and that patriotism is at a fever pitch. But the United States isn't the former Soviet Union, and the last thing Americans would want is that our press become the equivalent of the Soviet news agency Tass. President Bush's statement to other countries that "you're either with us or against us" doesn't apply to the media.

The war against terrorism could last years, if not decades. We need a free press to cover it.

Article 30

Bar Wars (Trial Lawyers are Not the Scourge of the Earth, Despite What the Prez Says) Philadelphia City Paper, August 12, 2004).

Like William Shakespeare, the Republican Party wants to kill all the trial lawyers. OK, Maybe it doesn't go that far, but it sure doesn't want one, namely Democratic Sen. John Edwards, to become vice president. During the past few years, Republicans have demonized trial lawyers and equated them to al-Qaeda and the Ku Klux Klan on the human food chain. It's becoming evident that the tort-reform debate between consumer and business interests will be on display throughout the campaign.

President Bush recently stated at a rally in Pittsburgh that he doesn't "think you can be pro-doc, pro-patient and pro-trial lawyer at the same time." In his recent "Girlyman" speech, California Gov. Arnold Schwarzenegger singled out trial lawyers as a problem. Two weeks ago, Vice President Dick Cheney gave a speech before doctors at an Ohio medical college during which he blamed trial lawyers for increased insurance costs.

Republicans claim that frivolous lawsuits brought by trial lawyers have resulted in runaway jury verdicts, thus resulting in higher medical costs and higher insurance premiums. As reviled as they might be, trial lawyers serve a valuable function in society. Lawsuits against major corporations, including HMOs and hospitals, help to keep these corporations in check. They act as consumer advocates and encourage the placement of safer products on the market.

If you want to slap an evil Darth Vader tag on someone, look no further than Bush and Cheney and their cozy relationships with big business and major corporations. Bush was part owner of the Texas Rangers baseball team and was a Texas oil businessman before being elected governor in 1994. Cheney ran the Halliburton oil-services company before resigning in 2000 to become Bush's running mate. Cheney receives more than $178,000 a year in deferred pay from Halliburton, which overbilled on multibillion-dollar, no-bid contracts to provide food and shelter to American troops in Iraq.

Corporate scandals have run rampant during the past few years, including the Enron bankruptcy. It's evident that the Bush-Cheney ticket cares more about protecting big business than providing health insurance to millions of uninsured Americans.

Modern-day America is becoming like America of the late 1800s, with greedy corporations and the emergence of monopolies.

Republicans might whine about trial lawyers, but if one of them gets in trouble with the law or is being investigated, who would be the first person they would call? After all, didn't Bush and Cheney rely on trial lawyers to help them win the election four years ago during the Florida recount?

Like in any profession, there are unethical, ambulance-chasing trial lawyers who give the field a bad name. Edwards and Sen. John Kerry support sanctions against plaintiffs and lawyers who bring frivolous medical malpractice suits.

However, many, if not most, trial lawyers fight for the underdog—injured victims and average consumers who otherwise wouldn't have any chance of being compensated for legitimate injuries.

During his career as a trial lawyer, Edwards was more like Luke Skywalker than Darth Vader. Sure, he made plenty of money, but he also took on cases to fight for the rights of average people as victims of defective products and medical malpractice. He represented a 5-year-old girl whose intestines were sucked into a swimming pool drain and a boy with cerebral palsy whose insurer refused to pay for therapy. Unlike Bush, a child of privilege who got every job he ever had due to his family's connections, Edwards earned his money on his own.

Tort reform might sound great, but much of it is a vehicle to protect large corporations and hurt the rights of injured consumers and limit their access to the judicial system. If it weren't for trial lawyers, who would serve as a check on the tobacco companies, asbestos manufacturers, manufacturers of defective tires and roll-over vehicles, and hospitals and doctors who commit medical malpractice?

So, if the Republicans want to make barristers a campaign issue, I say bring 'em on. May the Force be with the trial lawyer.

Article 31
States Must Eliminate Lead Poisoning (Baltimore Sun, Philadelphia City Paper, September 14, 2000)

For decades, it's been the stealth epidemic. Now, a battle is being waged to combat lead poisoning. But are we fighting the wrong enemy by going after the paint companies?

While the number of lead poisoning cases for children under age 6 has dropped from 14.8 million in 1978 (the year lead paint was banned) to 890,000 today, lead poisoning remains a serious problem. More than 7,000 children are exposed to lead paint in Baltimore each year, and 1,200 are poisoned. Poor children are five times more likely than others to have high blood-lead levels.

Unless the child of a famous athlete or actor is afflicted with lead paint poisoning, this issue will remain in the shadows of public opinion. There's no poster child to put a face on the disease, such as Michael J. Fox for Parkinson's Disease or Christopher Reeve for spinal cord injuries. Since this epidemic most affects the poor, no one seems to care.

Exposure to lead can lower IQ scores and cause learning disabilities and hyperactivity. High levels of lead in the blood can lead to brain damage, seizures, coma and death.

Bolstered by successful suits against the tobacco industry, many states and cities are trying to hold paint companies responsible for major damages and costs associated with lead poisoning. They hope to recover large amounts of money from paint companies through litigation to help pay for inspections and massive cleanups of lead from old homes and for screening young children for lead in their blood.

The litigation is similar to the attempts to hold tobacco companies and gun manufacturers liable for the injuries those products have caused in that they are trying to make the lead paint manufacturers responsible for lead poisoning. If these lawsuits, which are surfacing throughout the country, are successful, it would raise money for lead cleanups that either are not being carried out or are being conducted with insufficient federal, state and city dollars.

Unlike tobacco companies, however, paint companies no longer produce the harmful product because lead was banned from paint in 1978. Since the current paint companies no longer produce the harmful product, the imposition of liability is more difficult.

Many current lawsuits seek to hold paint manufacturers liable under a market-share liability theory.

Market-share liability is imposed on each industry member based on each member's percentage of the product placed on the market. The theory applies where all the named defendants are potential wrongdoers, the harmful products are identical and share the same defective qualities, plaintiffs cannot identify which defendant caused the injury and virtually all of the market manufacturers are named as defendants.

The theory was first used in a California Supreme Court case involving DES, an anti-miscarriage drug with an identical formula manufactured by several companies. But most courts, many in the East, have declined to apply market-share liability to lead paint manufacturers.

For example, a 1997 Pennsylvania Supreme Court case declined to apply market share liability to a lead paint case involving a home built in 1870, reasoning that from 1870 until the lead paint ban in 1978, several pigment manufacturers entered and left the lead paint market.

The Milwaukee City Council recently delayed voting on whether to file suit against the lead paint industry, reflecting a concern that similar suits have failed and that the suit would cost taxpayers millions in legal fees and take years to resolve.

While lawsuits against the lead paint industry have not succeeded, many lead poisoning victims have successfully sued landlords and property owners for negligence, breach of warranty of habitability and violations of consumer protection statutes.

Lead poisoning victims also have federal remedies. A mother recently sued the Philadelphia Housing Authority alleging that her home had lead paint in an amount 28 times over limits set by the U.S. Department of Housing and Urban Development (HUD). A federal judge denied the authority's motion to dismiss the mother's complaint that the agency violated HUD regulations.

In August, HUD announced that it will provide $104 million to enforce new lead-safety regulations to pay for lead tests and to expand lead abatement and inspection.

While children on Medicaid are supposed to be screened for lead at the age of 1 or 2, fewer than 20 percent nationwide are tested. Last year, Missouri sued two

Medicaid providers for breach of contract and Medicare fraud, alleging that the plans failed to screen their St. Louis pediatric patients for lead, as federal law requires.

Earlier this year, Maryland Gov. Parris N. Glendening and Baltimore Mayor Martin O'Malley pledged $50 million to address lead poisoning by enforcing lead paint violations, expanding blood screening programs and abating lead hazards in high risk housing. Maryland's legislature passed a bill requiring infants and toddlers in high-risk areas to be tested for lead poisoning.

Maryland's recent commitment is an example of why states should not rely solely on a tenuous market-share theory, which could take years to play out in courts. Painting black hats on the paint companies and vilifying them is not solving the immediate problem.

Instead, states should budget an extensive amount of money directly toward cleanups of old homes, screening of children, enforcing existing regulations regarding lead paint and public education.

We wiped out polio and many other diseases. Hopefully, through litigation, legislation, enforcement of regulations and education, we can eradicate the scourge of lead paint poisoning.

That's why one of the goals nationwide should be to prevent future lead poisoning incidents—not just by cleaning up lead from older homes but by funding ad campaigns and public service announcements promoting screening of infants as well as educating young children. And other states shouldn't wait for the war against paint companies to play out in the courts. They should follow Maryland's lead in directly trying to get the lead out.

Article 32
Law schools Fill Legal Aid Gap (Cleveland Plain Dealer, July 2, 1998. A revised version was published by the Detroit News)

Given the severe cutbacks in legal aid services over the last few years, how will the poor and indigent receive adequate legal representation? Many law schools, including several in Cleveland, are doing a great deal to help fill this gap.

Federal funding for civil legal aid was cut by 30 percent in 1996, forcing many programs to lay off staff and close branch offices. In February 1998, Legal Services Corp. officials went to Congress seeking $340 million in 1999 for civil legal aid for the poor. LSC estimates that 20 percent of Americans could be eligible for LSC—funded services because they are not able to pay for legal help. However, tens of thousands with critical legal problems are turned away because local programs lack enough staff and other resources to help them.

Cleveland-Marshall College of Law has a Street Law Program that allows law students to earn course credit while teaching law in area high schools. Its Fair Employment Practices Clinic provides credit for participation in litigation dealing with employment discrimination. Case Western Reserve University's Law School Clinic allows third-year students to represent low-income clients in civil and criminal cases, earning academic credit while providing a community service. Its Public Interest Law curriculum includes courses in employment discrimination, juvenile law and poverty, social inequality and the law.

The public service trend in legal education has become prevalent nationwide. Many Southwestern law schools have programs and clinicals focusing on providing legal services to American Indian communities. The University of New Mexico's American Indian Law Center has worked closely with the Navajo, Pueblo and other tribes to improve their judicial systems.

The University of Pennsylvania Law School established a mandatory public service program in 1990, which requires students to perform 70 hours of pro bono law-related services as a condition of graduation. During the academic year,

Penn law students perform more than 19,800 hours of service in more than 175 organizations at about 200 project sites. Seventy percent of the students work with low-income clients. Penn's program lets students provide services to the homeless or domestic violence victims, or perform research on death-penalty cases.

Contrary to popular belief, not everyone who goes to law school is looking to make six figures in a Wall Street law firm (not that there's anything wrong with that). Many law school applicants aspire to a career in which they actually can make a difference and change people's lives in a positive way.

Yes, there probably are too many lawyers in the United States, and there is fierce competition for jobs in the top law firms. Corporations and wealthy people can pick and choose among high-priced and well-known lawyers.

But poor people in this country have no such access to legal representation. There aren't enough lawyers, especially the "best and brightest," who choose public-interest law as a career. In many cases, the choice to pass up a public-service career in favor of a comfortable, big-law-firm existence is a necessary financial one. Many, if not most, law school graduates accrue school loan debts of close to $100,000, which take years to pay off.

The law schools' loan forgiveness programs, public-interest scholarships and pro bono clinical programs give future lawyers a realistic chance to realize their dreams of being public-interest crusaders and servants of the needy. Many no longer have to laugh, cry or shake their heads when they see a job placement ad for a public-service organization or legal aid clinic that can offer only a $15,000 annual salary.

But even those who choose traditional law firms or corporate positions can benefit from public-service clinical programs in law school. Their experiences during these clinicals might open their eyes to a world of the neglected and ignored that will stay with them for the rest of their careers. They might become more inclined to volunteer for pro bono legal services and, once they become experienced attorneys and partners, can influence their firms to provide more pro bono hours of service to the poor.

As a nation that promises "liberty and justice for all," we have a long way to go to ensure that the poor get their day in court.

Law schools, however, can help fill this need and, at the same time, influence a future generation of lawyers to give at least some of their time to those who need legal services but cannot afford them.

Article 33
Ways to Surf the Internet Safely (Philadelphia Inquirer, February 15, 1997)

The tragic slaying of a suburban Philadelphia woman engaged in flirting on the Internet has demonstrated the dangers of seeking cyberspace relationships. But, as yet, there are no standard guidelines about Internet ethics or the social ramifications involved with this new technology.

One place to start is in school. Pennsylvania should mandate that school districts establish "acceptable use" policies for their students, who should be given at least one seminar a year on the social and ethical issues surrounding the Net.

In an article in the August 1996 School Library Journal, media specialist Rebecca Palgi provided a blueprint: Use rules should set forth the rights, responsibilities and risks of online resources, establish penalties for students who fail to follow guidelines, and obtain parental consent for the students' use of online access. She suggests that both students and parents be required to sign agreements indicating that they understand the guidelines for online access and take full responsibility for compliance.

Some schools already have taken steps. In the Lower Merion School District, the teaching of computer ethics has been an important part of the curriculum for some time. The district passed an acceptable use policy last year and is working on a set of specific guidelines that will be given to students and parents. Parents will receive these guidelines through mailed brochures. And students will receive special training as to the social and ethical implications of the Internet—and the penalties for misuse.

The Philadelphia school district has put such policies in place at the teacher level. Teachers are trained in Internet ethics as part of their professional development and are expected to share the information with students. But no parental consent is necessary for student use of the Internet, and there are no mandated ethics classes for students.

There are plenty of social and ethical issues to cover, such as keeping children from obtaining pornography, advising people that many of the documents that appear on the Internet are copyrighted, and telling students to meet online friends in person only in public places like a restaurant or a bookstore. There are also issues of security, etiquette and harassment.

True, some of this might be common sense—most 13-year-olds would know that it would be wrong to blow up their school by using instructions from the Internet on how to build pipe bombs—but it helps to be exposed to hypothetical situations.

Internet training in schools could be modeled after continuing legal education courses and other ethics programs for professionals such as doctors and accountants. Pennsylvania mandates that attorneys complete 12 hours of such programs each year, including a minimum of one hour on ethics and professionalism.

Training in ethics and other issues of the Internet can't cover everything in a limited amount of time, but it can expose students on an ongoing basis to real-world problems, both anticipated and unanticipated.

Right now, Internet usage is a free-for-all. There should be clear ground rules established so that people, especially kids, can have a safe, fun and educational ride while surfing the Net and can learn how to avoid the sharks and other pitfalls lurking in this Brave New World.

Article 34
Now's the Time to Relive Live Aid II (Philadelphia and New York Metro, December 2, 2004)

For decades, Woodstock has been the concert that everyone cherishes and wants to live over and over. In 1994 and 1999, there were even more days of peace, sex, drugs, and rock and roll. However, there's another concert that took place a few years ago that should be celebrated and duplicated once again. Next summer will be the 20 th Anniversary of Live Aid.

A DVD box set of the 1985 concert was released in November, with the proceeds going to charity. Bob Geldof and co-organiser Midge Ure just released an updated CD of the 1984 Band Aid charity single "Do They Know It's Christmas?," featuring artists such as Robbie Williams and Coldplay's Chris Martin.

Twenty years ago, the world was focused on Philadelphia and London, for Live Aid, the megaconcert for African famine relief. For 16 hours, the world was a global village, as 1.5 billion television viewers in 160 countries saw superstars such as U2, Paul McCartney, Eric Clapton, Madonna, and a reunited Led Zeppelin dazzle capacity crowds at Wembley Stadium and JFK Stadium. The concert raised millions of dollars for famine relief in Ethiopia.

For those of you who in Mullet Nation who went to Live Aid, as I did, doesn't it seem like only yesterday? Memories of the Mick Jagger and Tina Turner duet; the "surprise" Crosby, Stills, Nash, and Young reunion; Phil Collins jetting across the Atlantic to perform at both venues; firehoses sprayed on the crowd to ease the sweltering heat; flooded bathrooms that resembled conditions of third world countries; and the Philly crowd booing the Soviet rock group Autograph as they appeared on huge television screens via satellite—not because they represented the evil USSR, but because they were pretty bad.

Like Woodstock, it was music and fun and a bunch of drugs. (I did not inhale the second-hand smoke, by the way). But, it was music with a social conscience and charitable purpose.

So why has no Live Aid II been organized? Is it that most of Live Aid's stars are past their prime? Generation X apathy towards social causes? Absence of a motivated organizer like Bob Geldof?

Musicians and grandiose concerts can't bail us out of all our social dilemmas. But, events like Live Aid raise social consciousness and money, without government involvement or raising taxes.

The time is ripe for Live Aid II. Much of Africa suffers from poverty, conflict, and famine. Swarms of locusts have caused grain shortages in Mali, and there is a predicted famine in Ethiopia in 2005. Refugees are fleeing violence in the Sudan and living in camps in Chad. Money and donations have been sent, but this is an ongoing problem. Unlike Woodstock '99 and Woodstock '94, Live Aid II wouldn't be a mere effort for promoters to make money.

The original Woodstock was a sociological phenomenon. Woodstock '94 and '99 were greedy capitalist endeavors. In contrast, Live Aid saved lives. It is the spirit of Live Aid, not Woodstock, that should be emulated, copied, and held sacred. Since the concert, the Live Aid Foundation and Band Aid Trust has spent over $144 million on African relief projects.

The world needs Live Aid II a lot more than it needs another Woodstock. We can feed the world again.

Article 35
It's Time to Give Africa Some Live Debt Aid,
(Philadelphia and New York Metro, June 2, 2005)

Another Live Aid? Didn't we feed the world 20 years ago?

We did. But Africa is still hungry. In fact, it's starving.

At this week's Live 8 press conference, concert organizer Bob Geldof stated that a child dies in Africa from hunger, AIDS, or inadequate health care every three seconds. Geldof stated that although the 1985 Live Aid concert raised over $200 million, "…that's the amount that Africa pays in interest on its debt service every five days."

According to Debt Aids Trade Africa (DATA), an organization that was co-founded by Bono, U2's lead singer, 9,500 Africans are infected with HIV/AIDS every day and 200 million people go hungry every day. At least one million Africans, most of them young children, will die of malaria and two million will die of AIDS. Thus far, 17 million Africans have died from AIDS. According to the Belfast Telegraph, poverty kills 50,000 Africans per day.

It's not as though recent efforts haven't been made to try to help Africa.

Recently, Bono and a host of prominent entertainers, celebrities, and politicians formed the One Campaign, which was launched last year in Philadelphia and is Bono's latest attempt to help Africa and third-world countries. His organization, DATA, works to raise awareness of the crisis facing Africa and to increase support in the United States and abroad to increase funding and promote policies which will benefit Africa. It also informs citizens of wealthier countries and tries to increase grassroots support for better policies towards Africa. Among DATA's goals is to fight the AIDS crisis through raising money and providing needed drugs, providing more development assistance, and urging wealthy countries around the world to relieve the unpayable debts of African countries.

Despite these efforts, something bigger was needed. The devastation in Africa is equivalent to an ongoing Tsunami. The world responded generously to last year's Tsunami disaster, and it needs to respond again.

As Geldof indicated, Live 8 isn't out to raise money; its goal is to influence and persuade President Bush and other leaders of wealthy Western nations who will meet at the July G8 summit in Scotland to cancel Africa's enormous and unpayable debts, double aid for the continent, and make trade fair.

According to the Guardian (UK), Great Britain's Prime Minister Tony Blair is trying to convince President Bush "not to risk the wrath of Europe by holding out on a deal to lift the debt burdens on Africa."

If the United States can find a way to pay over $200 billion and counting to "liberate" Iraq in a war that was based on faulty intelligence, don't we have a moral obligation to liberate an entire continent that has to endure unimaginable suffering and poverty? Quite frankly, most of the people attending the five Live 8 concerts in London, Philadelphia, Paris, Rome, and Berlin could care less about the cause. They'll just be looking to have a great time and enjoy performances from many prominent musicians.

Hopefully, world leaders and decision makers will get the message behind the music. Charitable donations haven't been enough to Feed the World. It's time for the nations of the world to step up to the plate so that the people of Africa can finally have food on their plate.

Article 36
Don't sell Folk Festival short with tired stereotypes of folkies; There is a diversity of fan age groups and musical styles. It's all positive. (Philadelphia Inquirer, August 26, 2004)

I used to be a Philadelphia Folk Festival skeptic. In high school, I remember seeing the band-camp kids wearing Folk Festival T-shirts with the banjo with the smiley face at the end and thinking, "This seems pretty lame."

Some people's image of the Folk Festival might be of a bunch of toothless hillbillies pickin' and a grinnin' while playing to a Hee-Haw audience of Junior Samples and Grandpa Jones-types. However, when I attended my first festival in 1992, I became hooked instantly. I've gone back almost every year since, and when the festival has its three-day run starting tomorrow, I'll be there. It's a great way to get in touch with my inner hippie.

Based in Schwenksville, Montgomery County, the festival is sort of a PG-rated Woodstock. There are no naked people, but lots in tie-dye T-shirts. People bring their families, and there is Dulcimer Grove, a large area for children's songs, jugglers, face painting, arts and crafts, and storytelling. In the crafts area, you can watch demonstrations by candlemakers, glassblowers and blacksmiths. During the day, there's music on five stages, and then there is a main afternoon and evening concert.

Since its beginning in 1962, the festival has attracted such big names as Los Lobos, Janis Ian, Mary Chapin Carpenter, Judy Collins, Pete Seeger, John Sebastian, Richie Havens and Arlo Guthrie. This year's performers include Kris Kristofferson and Taj Mahal. However, I like seeing new artists whom I've never heard of—such as Tempest and Alice Peacock—and thinking, "They should be famous."

The festival features musical genres from across the world. I've seen performers from Australia, Canada and South Africa. In recent years, the festival has added dance tents, where you can learn contra, square, Cajun, polka, salsa,

English and Irish dances. And while the festival has modernized some things over the years, such as its shuttle bus system and food concession tents, you still might want to bring a flashlight for use when you go to the Porta-Potty late at night.

So what exactly is folk music?

"You can ask any five people up in Schwenksville and get five different definitions," said local singer/songwriter John Flynn, who has performed six times at the festival since 1995. "I think of it as music you didn't pay someone to teach you. It comes to you due to love. For me, it's a way to vent, and say things from the heart."

Gene Shay, a festival cofounder, said a precise definition is impossible. "It's songs about the human condition…. It's more of a feeling than music. Unlike pop music, it's about we, not I, me, mine." Folk music has a long tradition of protest and social relevance, with Woody Guthrie, Pete Seeger, the Weavers, Joan Baez, and Peter, Paul and Mary among its chief practitioners. "When people live in troublesome times, folk music becomes more relevant," Shay said. "Artists write about society's woes, but also have a message of change and 'We shall overcome.'"

After years of frivolous bubble-gum music manufactured by Britney Spears, 'N Sync, et. al., folk music is regaining relevance. Said Flynn: "For a long time, folk music became introspective. Now, folk music is once again reaching out to people, addressing the human condition." One of the festival's attributes is the diversity of age groups. Another is the positive vibe. There are group sings in the campgrounds; about 5,000 festivalgoers camp out for the weekend. Others, like me, just go up for an afternoon or evening concert.

In some ways, the Folk Festival is like the Betsy Ross House or Liberty Bell—a local treasure that many in the area have never visited. I can't remember how many times I've asked people whether they've been to the event and they say, "You know, I always wanted to go to it, but I've never made it up there."

What makes the Philadelphia Folk Festival so special and different from others? "There's nothing like it across the country as far as the spirit, diversity, level of artists, and crowds," Flynn said.

Shay said the feeling of family and community makes the festival special. "Other festivals are attended by lots of detached individuals," he said. "Our festival has evolved into a little village where friends reunite every year."

Article 37
From Computer Meek to Geezer Geek (Computers and the Elderly) (San Francisco Chronicle, 2000. A revised version was published in the Baltimore Sun)

My mother has become one of the "Geezer Geeks." Computer geek, that is. She uses her computer to e-mail friends in Florida, to research travel spots, get restaurant menus and information on cosmetic and beauty products.

My mother (I'm sworn to "Survivor"-type secrecy about her age) is not alone, but there should be many more older people who use computers. For a large number of these people, computers can serve as a vital link to the outside world.

Seniors are the fastest-growing group of Internet users in America, according to International Data Corp., a worldwide research firm. More than 12 million seniors are online, a 106-percent increase from 1999. But only 1 in 8 Americans age 65 and older uses the Internet, according to the Pew Research Center's Internet Project.

Last year, a Department of Commerce study showed that 67 percent of Americans over 65 have never used a computer, as reported in the Record, northern New Jersey. While 75 percent of people between 18 and 29 have Internet access, only 15 percent of people over 75 have such access. Jupiter Communications, a New York tech firm, predicts that while 17 million Americans over 50 will be surfing the Web by 2005, 36 million will not.

Too many seniors, such as my 79-year-old father, are the "Computer Meek." When I asked my father if his assisted-living facility would ever consider bringing in computers for residents, he laughed and said, "That idea wouldn't go over too well there—most of the residents are half asleep all day."

Like most elderly people, his philosophy is, "What do I need a computer for? If I want to talk to somebody, I'll pick up a phone." Despite the skepticism of many of their peers, a growing number of senior citizens are learning how to use computers.

SeniorNet, a nonprofit organization, is the world's largest teacher of computer skills for people 50 and older, with more than 200 learning centers in 38 states. The average age of SeniorNet's 39,000 members is 69.

"Generations on Line" is a nonprofit group in Philadelphia whose goal is to introduce seniors to the Internet. MyGait, a Houston company, installs computers modified for seniors in retirement homes and sells computer services to retirement homes.

One of the barriers to computer use by the elderly is their fear of new and complicated technology. In response, tech companies have introduced devices, such as Web-TV and I-Opener, which let users send e-mail and surf the Web without having to master the complexity of computers.

Agespan, an Atlanta company dedicated to helping seniors with new technology, recently unveiled "Ginger," a new user-friendly touch-screen and voice-operated personal computer for seniors. Computer-wired homes could help senior citizens remain independent by giving them Internet access to buy books, order groceries, obtain health information and get their prescriptions filled.

Already, there are Web sites dedicated to senior issues and opinions, care-giving resources, legal issues such as probate matters, senior magazines, travel, retirement financial planning, health and diseases, nutrition and government agencies of interest to seniors.

It's ironic that the most frequent users of computers are young people, who should be outside playing sports, traveling, hiking, and going to nightclubs, concerts and dances.

Meanwhile, elderly people, particularly those who can't drive at night or are physically infirm or disabled, would benefit the most from using computers as a lifeline to the outside world.

It's a tough sell to convert people like my father from a Computer Meek to a Geezer Geek. But who knows? If technology companies can weave a less-tangled Web, maybe I'll be able to send him a virtual card online for his 80th birthday.

Article 38
We Need a Market to Rival Faneuil Hall
(Philadelphia Inquirer, August 30, 1994)

The city recently launched a pilot program intended to liven up Independence National Historical Park-complete with town criers, banners, new tours, and dramatic historical performances. It's a nice start, but it's not enough.

What the area needs is a colonial-style marketplace and a vibrant performance area.

Historical sites can be preserved and even enhanced by commercial activity. Take Boston's Faneuil Hall and Quincy Market.

Faneuil Hall was constructed in 1742 as an open market and a meeting space suitable for town gatherings. After 252 years it is still the most popular spot in Boston for both tourists and locals. After major reconstruction in the 1970s, the hall and the adjacent Quincy Market now contain more than 100 shops and pushcarts as well as scores of restaurants and cafes and a food court the length of almost two football fields.

The meeting room at Faneuil Hall still serves as a public meeting place, hosting debates on national and community issues, high school graduations and naturalization ceremonies. The marketplace area bustles with activity day and night and features free street performances from varied artists such as jugglers, bagpipe players and acrobatic dancers. Of course, the Faneuil Hall-Quincy Market area is far too modern and trendy to present a precise model for an Independence Mall marketplace. Picture instead a rustic working marketplace, where numerous artisans sell goods and provide demonstrations.

This outdoor marketplace would be authentic, tasteful, and respectful of the past. Instead of pizza and eggrolls, the Independence Mall marketplace would serve exclusively colonial fare-fresh baked bread, scones, hardtack, teas, Yorkshire pudding, ginger cookies, molasses beer, etc. Instead of stores hawking T-shirts and pennants, our mall would have booths of various artisans such as blacksmiths, glassblowers, and metalcrafters. All marketplace employees would wear colonial attire.

The emphasis would be on the visitor walking from booth to booth to see the demonstrations of how the food was prepared and how the crafts were made. Sale of the food and goods made would be tangential to the marketplace's primary purpose, which would be to provide a realistic 18th century experience.

Generally, the National Park Service frowns upon commercial activity. However, it is permitted where it is deemed necessary and appropriate to protect park lands.

An example of merging history and commercial enterprise in national parks already exists here. City Tavern, located at Second and Walnut, was built by the Park Service in 1976 as a replica of the original City Tavern, which was the Founding Fathers' favorite gathering place. The tavern is owned and supervised by the Park Service and is run by a private concessionaire.

The tavern's mission is to provide an authentic 18th Century culinary experience. Waitresses clothed in colonial attire serve fare such as country rabbit terrine, pepperpot soup, and medallions of venison. Musicians dressed in period costumes play harp, flute and violin to complement the dining experience.

Admittedly, area merchants might object to any commercial activity on the mall. However, the mall's primary customers would be tourists, just like those who now patronize the City Tavern. And nobody claims it lures business from the Delaware Avenue clubs. City residents and area workers aren't going to go to the mall to get some Yorkshire pudding for lunch; they're more apt to patronize the many restaurants at the Reading Terminal market or a fast-food restaurant at the Gallery.

As for the amphitheater at Judge Lewis Quadrangle, it should either be emphasized or rebuilt as a featured performance site. It should host daily concerts of 18th century music-i.e., harpsichord concerts, choral performances and classical music recitals.

There should be historical debates between colonial figures on the issues of the late 18th century, some perhaps loosely based on the Federalist Papers. Create a "Constitution for kids"-daily skits, performances, and interactive shows specifically designed for school age children that focus on the Constitution and how it applies today.

From the amphitheater, a fife and drum procession could circle around the park area throughout the day.

If Philadelphia wants to be something other than a one-day pit stop for tourists between New York and Washington, it must do something bold and special with its centerpiece attraction. I'm not talking about Disneyizing the park or cheapening its pristine image, but it needs excitement.

Article 39
Yet Another Flood of Beatlemania Leaves Fans Wishing For a Reunion (Philadelphia Inquirer and Baltimore Sun, November 9, 2000.

Everyone seems to be taking a ticket to ride on the new round of Beatlemania.

In September, the three surviving Beatles re-released the movie "Yellow Submarine" and a new accompanying CD. A few months later, Paul McCartney played a concert at the Cavern Club in Liverpool, the site of the Beatles' early rise to fame. During the summer, the Beatles provided "Help!" (the movie) to be part of a Beatles movie collection on DVD.

Paul's forthcoming album will include "Free Now," which was released to British radio stations recently and includes outtakes from the Beatles' recording sessions in the late 1960s. In the fall, the surviving members of the Fab Four will publish a book documenting the group's history.

This is not making me twist and shout with glee. Don't get me wrong. I love the Beatles. It's just that the repackaging of old material and their decision to remain apart is the equivalent of feeding their fans crumbs. I won't be satisfied until I get a full course meal—a live concert with the three surviving Beatles.

At 39 years old, I'm a "tweener"—not old enough to be a baby boomer but too old to fall into Generation X. I was 3 when the Beatles invaded America and appeared on Ed Sullivan for the first time. I was 5 when they stopped doing live concerts. Since my parents' musical tastes favored Bing Crosby and Robert Goulet, I didn't get to experience artists like Jimi Hendrix, The Who and Jefferson Airplane.

Yet the Beatles transcended all musical tastes and were played on almost every AM radio station. I remember being captivated when "Hey, Jude" was released in August, 1968. I cried when I heard the news reports in 1970 that the Beatles had broken up.

For many in my generation, we kept waiting in the 1970s for what we thought would be the inevitable Beatles reunion. The anticipation reached ridiculous extremes. I remember one syndicated program that would simulate a Beatles concert by playing Beatles songs with fake crowd noise in the background. Lorne Michaels of "Saturday Night Live" had a running skit parodying this frenzy by offering the Beatles $3,000 if they would reunite on the show.

Even after the death of John Lennon in 1980, the clamor for a Beatles reunion continued. In 1996, the three remaining Beatles had a semi-reunion with their "Anthology" series. While the remaining Beatles played in a recording studio, it didn't have the closure that their fans sought.

In the past 10 years, Paul McCartney put out solo albums such as "Flaming Pie," George Harrison performed with the Traveling Wilburys, and Ringo Starr toured with his "All-Starr Band." Yet, even though Paul and George still have excellent voices, they have declined to get together to perform Beatles songs.

I can't get excited about the re-mixing and re-issuing of old songs complete with high-tech enhancements and perhaps a line or two stated in a different manner. And, Paul playing solo just doesn't energize most people these days.

Critics of any sort of Beatles' reunion might say "Let it be. They could never recapture the excitement of the 1960s concerts, and they might even come across as pathetic old geezers. Gee, are they going to play 'When I'm 64?'" Well, their fellow oldsters, the Rolling Stones, still give their fans satisfaction and sell out large stadiums. Santana's still smooth and Crosby, Stills, Nash, and Young are still rockin' the free world.

George, Paul and Ringo should just suck it up and do what the whole world has been clamoring for during the past 30 years: hold one major farewell concert in London or New York. Let it be on pay-per-view, with the proceeds going to charities such as breast cancer research in memory of Linda McCartney, organizations for the hungry and homeless (George organized the concert for Bangladesh in the early '70s), or AIDS research. Have guest performers such as Peter Frampton, Eric Clapton, Elton John and Julian and Sean Lennon.

I've seen a lot of live rock concerts over the years, yet I always lament that I, along with the rest of my generation and the ones that followed it, never got to see the greatest rock group in history perform on stage.

Come together, lads. Now.

Article 40
U2 Does Well As Bono Does Good (Philadelphia Daily News, May 14, 2005)

Saturday May 14 th and Sunday May 22nd will be Beautiful Days for Philly fans of the Irish rock group U2, which will play at the Wachovia Center as part of the Vertigo Tour.

In March, U2 was inducted into the Rock and Roll Hall Fame. Deservedly so. As far as rock bands go, U2 deserves to be on Mount Rushmore, along with The Beatles, The Who, and The Rolling Stones. The Beatles were like the baseball equivalent of Sandy Koufax—six or seven dominant years of musical genius. After they split up, they enjoyed pretty good careers. U2 is more like Steve Carlton or Warren Spahn—consistent excellence over 22 years.

The band consists of Bono (Paul Hewson), the Edge (Dave Evans), Adam Clayton, and Larry Mullen. They released their first album "Boy" in 1980 and then "October" in 1981, but their breakthrough album came in 1983 with "War," which featured the hit songs "Sunday Bloody Sunday" and "New Years Day." They have two current hits off of their new album, "How to Dismantle an Atomic Bomb."

What makes U2 stand out musically from the crowd is their excellence and relevance over such a long time span. No other rock band can match U2 in this regard. The Stones were great and they still put on a good show, but they haven't had a hit album since Tattoo You in 1981. The Who hasn't released a studio album since 1982, and they've spent more time apart than together since then.

It's remarkable that U2, a bunch of guys in their mid-40s, still connect so intensely with their fans. The first set of Vertigo Tour shows in Philadelphia in May sold out the 20,000-seat Wachovia Center in around 15 minutes. The second set of tickets for two U2 shows in September sold out in around two hours.

It was the Live Aid concert in 1985, however, that catapulted U2 into superstar status. It's appropriate that a humanitarian band stole the show at a humanitarian event.

What makes U2 stand out in a more important way is their humanitarianism. Lots of bands and musical artists play charity concerts. However, U2 has emerged as this generation's voice of social conscience through their music and their deeds. While he's not there yet, Bono is on his way to becoming as significant a historic world figure as Mother Teresa, Nelson Mandela, and Martin Luther King. At a minimum, he's equaled the energy and social conscience of John Lennon. Bono is believed to be one of the 144 nominees for this year's Nobel Peace Prize.

Recently, Bono and a host of prominent entertainers, celebrities, and politicians formed the One Campaign, which was launched last year in Philadelphia and is Bono's latest attempt to help Africa and third-world countries. Bono is the co-founder of Debt Aids Trade Africa (DATA), an organization that works to raise awareness of the crisis facing Africa and to increase support in the United States and abroad to increase funding and promote policies which will benefit Africa. It also informs citizens of wealthier countries and tries to increase grassroots support for better policies towards Africa. Among DATA's goals is to fight the AIDS crisis through raising money and providing needed drugs, providing more development assistance, and urging wealthy countries around the world to relieve the unpayable debts of African countries.

In explaining how he got involved with social causes, Bono told the Technology, Entertainment, and Design Conference in February that his journey began in 1985, the summer of Live Aid, when he and his wife worked at an orphanage in Ethiopia for a month. "We found Africa to be a magical place—big skies, big hearts, big shining continent, beautiful royal people.... Anyway, on our last day at this orphanage, a man handed me his baby and said, "Would you take my son with you?" And he knew in Ireland that his son would live, and that in Ethiopia, his son would die. It was the middle of that awful famine. Well, I turned him down, and it was a funny kind of sick feeling, but I turned him down, and it's a feeling I can't ever quite forget. And, in that moment, I started this journey. In that moment, I became the worst thing of all. I became a rock star with a cause."

Since then, Bono has been focusing on countries where the Streets Have No Name (assuming that there are any streets at all).

Many people believe that musicians and entertainers should just shut up and play music, not preach about various social causes. They also assert that these artists are out of the mainstream and won't influence the public.

However, after a long era of Britney Spears and N'Sync-type of bubble gum frivolity, musicians are once again becoming socially relevant and speaking out against injustice. There's a strong tradition of this, such as Woody Guthrie's

political and social songs of protest, Vietnam protest songs, the No Nukes concerts, Live Aid, and Amnesty International. Throughout the years, musicians
have proven that music can make a difference.

You may say that Bono's a dreamer. But hopefully he's not the only one.

Article 41

Never Muzak, Forever Rock and Roll (Philadelphia Inquirer, June 21, 2005. Revised versions appeared in the Baltimore Sun and Orange County Register)

Even though I'm only 44 years old, there are many signs that I'm starting to get old.

My knees ache from arthritis and I limp like Walter Brennan after I play basketball. My eyesight and hearing is diminishing, as is my hairline.

But perhaps one of the clearest signs that I'm getting older is the fact that the music I grew up listening to has evolved into elevator music.

While eating at various fast food restaurants during the past couple of years, I've heard Muzak versions of Eric Clapton's "Let it Rain," Jethro Tull's "Bungle in the Jungle," and Led Zeppelin's "Stairway to Heaven." The music that we considered radical, cool, and hip has now been sanitized and repackaged as bland background music. The music that kids inhaled marijuana smoke to is now the music we inhale french fries to.

Twenty years from now, will Burger King be playing graphic stuff such as "Closer" by Nine Inch Nails? I haven't heard the Beatles' Helter Skelter yet, but that might be coming to a mall or grocery store near you soon.

When I'm at the optometrist, I don't want to hear a Muzak version of "Doctor My Eyes" by Jackson Browne. I'm not sure what would be more painful during a dental visit—the drill, or listening to a Muzak version of U2's "Sunday Bloody Sunday." "Rebel, Rebel" by David Bowie and the Beatles' "Revolution" just doesn't have the same effect when it's being played by violins instead of guitars.

Growing up as a kid in the 1970s, the oldies radio station would play artists from the 1950s like Elvis Presley and Fats Domino. Now, the oldies stations are playing the music from my youth—The Who, The Police, and Bruce Springsteen.

I suppose that some of today's pop music will lend itself well to Muzak in the future. To my old, jaded tastes, Justin Timberlake and Kelly Clarkson sound like Muzak already. Even with current musical groups that I like, I can still see Muzak potential for groups and artists like Keane, Coldplay, and John Mayer.

Rock and roll is supposed to be wild, subversive, and controversial. It arouses passion, emotion, and memories. It breaks my heart to hear it in its neutered form. It's also a slap in the face to realize that the music you thought was so cool isn't cool anymore and is now considered Jurassic.

A couple years ago, I attended a wedding of a couple who were in their 70s. At the reception, they played Neil Diamond and Barbra Streisand CD's. While most of the guests were in their 70s and 80s, I was at the kids' table with people ranging from teenagers to age 40. While the oldsters were singing along with the tunes, the music was making us youngsters gag and we had to restrain ourselves from getting up and hurling the CD player against the wall. This wasn't our party and we just had to deal with it. Thirty years from now, young people will be sitting at a wedding, listening to Sting and Dave Matthews Band CD's and griping about how lame the music is.

I still love to listen to classic groups and artists like the Beatles, the Who, the Rolling Stones, and Billy Joel—it's still rock and roll to me. Unfortunately, to others, it has become the Sound of Muzak.

Article 42
A Reunion Reminds Us The Death Of Disco Is Something To Dance About (Philadelphia Inquirer, June 3, 2000).

Spring isn't just time for graduation; it's also a popular time for high school and college reunions-a time to see old friends and to relive the era in which you grew up. Unfortunately, I grew up during the much-maligned 1970s.

Last year, I went to my 20th year high school reunion. For months, I had been looking forward to seeing old friends as well as seeing who looked the same and who, like me, had become candidates for Rogaine or the Atkins diet (no relation, by the way).

As it turned out, the reunion was enjoyable. Except for two things-the girl who I had tried to date for four years still gave me short shrift, and I had to listen to disco music for four hours.

The pimply teenage disc jockeys probably meant well. They figured that they would keep the old geezers happy by playing the whole Saturday Night Fever album. I had hoped for hot hors d'oeuvres; I wasn't expecting a disco inferno.

In retrospect, the 70s have been characterized as the disco decade. In reality, disco was a short term fad, almost an extended version of the Macarena in the 90s. This was especially true for kids like me growing up in a suburban high school, where Disco Fever was a mere head cold.

Most kids at Cheltenham High School in suburban Philadelphia in the 70s didn't dress up like Donna Summer or John Travolta in Saturday Night Fever. Most of us didn't listen to the Bee Gees. Disco Duck? Nope. We ducked disco. Unlike the Village People, we didn't want to be Macho Men or stay at the YMCA.

Picture instead the kids in the movies Dazed and Confused and Fast Times at Ridgemont High. Our album racks (I think there might still be some of those at the Smithsonian) were filled with Led Zeppelin, the Eagles, the Grateful Dead, Eric Clapton, and Lynyrd Skynyrd. The concerts we went to were Springsteen, the Who, Yes, and Genesis. The late 70s also saw the beginning of so-called modern rock with emerging artists such as Elvis Costello and the Police. While disco was popular in large American cities, it never really caught fire in the suburbs. According to Rolling Stone Magazine's Encyclopedia of Rock and Roll, disco first emerged in the mid-1970s from New York's gay male culture, and it did not reach a mass audience until 1977, when the Saturday Night Fever soundtrack sold 20 million copies. All-disco radio stations began earning top ratings in urban areas; disco-influenced fashion, such as spandex, became popular; and some rock and roll acts, such as Queen, Rod Stewart, and the Rolling Stones put out disco-influenced hits. But the disco supernova burned out quickly by 1980, as the public rarely made a long-term identification with disco's biggest stars.

I remember the one time that I caved in and let a couple of my friends who were in their six-month disco phase drag me kicking and screaming to a disco in Northeast Philly. I've had better dental visits. I felt like the one normal human being amongst a roomful of aliens in Invasion of the Body Snatchers.

Unfortunately, it's often a fringe culture that defines an entire generation. In the 50s, more kids probably looked like Richie Cunningham and Wally Cleaver, yet in retrospect, we think that everyone was a greaser and looked and dressed like James Dean or the "Fonz." In the 60s, the hippie culture ran from the summer of 1967 until the end of the decade, but not everyone dressed up in love beads and tie-dye t-shirts. Similarly, most of today's kids don't dye their hair blue or have multiple tattoos and body piercing. Twenty years from now, will today's kids want their 20th year reunion to be a four hour "rave?" I don't think so.

In retrospect, we have glorified disco and forgotten how popular the "anti-disco" sentiment was. In 1979, the Chicago White Sox had a "disco demolition" night, at which almost 50,000 fans chanted "Disco Sucks," hundreds of disco records were burned, and fans rioted on the field. By the time I started La Salle University in 1979, there was only one kid in the entire dorm complex, "Disco Dave," a 98-pound, tough talking waif from the Bronx, who embraced the disco culture. Rock music was played exclusively in the dorm rooms and at all the college parties. Like many others, as I've gotten older, my musical tastes have expanded from only rock and roll to jazz, blues, classical, and folk. But through the years, my hatred of disco has remained constant. Nothing personal, but (as KC and the Sunshine Band would say) that's the way, uh-huh, uh-huh, I like it.

Article 43
Forget About Saddam, Let's Focus on Al-Qaeda (OpEdNews.com, a liberal Internet publication, December 2003).

OK. We got him.

Obviously, the capture of Saddam Hussein is a significant boost to the United States' effort to rebuild Iraq and was a magnificent achievement by the American military forces. However, it still doesn't diminish the reality that the Bush administration's ill-conceived American adventure in Iraq is voodoo foreign policy and a sideshow to the real fight against terrorism.

To paraphrase James Carville and the Clinton war room, "It's about Al Qaeda, stupid." Our invasion of Iraq and deposing of Saddam might be good public relations, but as far as fighting terror, it was the equivalent of bombing China after the Japanese attacked Pearl Harbor in 1941.

Saddam was not an imminent threat to the United States, there were no ties to Al Qaeda, there is still no evidence of weapons of mass destruction, and we failed to organize a broad worldwide coalition in this war. Iran and Syria have much stronger ties to terrorists, yet at this point, we've left them alone.

American society is parochial and inward looking. Most Americans are becoming complacent, since there haven't been any post 9–11 attacks on American soil. Many Americans will likely feel safer now that Saddam has been captured, but in reality, we're not. A federal advisory commission recently warned that federal resources and attention from homeland terrorism preparedness have been distracted and lost momentum. Once again, the nation is at an Orange alert.

How soon many of us have forgotten that Al-Qaeda has masterminded several attacks of terrorism during the last two years, including Bali, Turkey, Saudi Arabia, and Morocco.

Published reports have indicated that the United States has diverted its attention, manpower, and funding from fighting terrorists in Afghanistan to Iraq. As

Reuters reported last week, the Taliban is actively operating in Pakistan. Last week, an assassination attempt of Pakistan President Musharraf barely missed. A recent video sent to the BBC showed that Taliban fighters are roaming freely in southern Afghanistan. Hopefully, now that the Saddam sideshow is over, we can refocus our efforts on the real enemy, Al Qaeda.

According to a recent Washington Post article, Al-Qaeda is still receiving a significant amount of funding and governments around the world are not doing nearly enough to enforce global sanctions and curb the terror group's financial resources. Experts believe Osama bin Laden is located on the mountainous border of Afghanistan and Pakistan and that he is being protected by local tribesmen. The humiliating capture of Saddam and any subsequent punishment, including the death penalty, will not have any deterring effect on Al-Qaeda.

There is an analogy between the celebration of Iraqis after the fall of Baghdad and last week's celebration over the capture of Saddam Hussein.

No doubt that conservative pundits will beat their chests and proclaim "Mission Accomplished," just like they did after the fall of Baghdad to gloat that they were right about invading Iraq. Their gloating will once again be premature. There is still a great deal of anti-American sentiment throughout the Arab world, the insurgent attacks in Iraq are likely to continue, and there is a risk that an Islamic fundamentalist state could rise from democratic elections in Iraq.

Obviously, Saddam Hussein was a brutal dictator who had a tyrannical reign over Iraq. However, despite all the hype, he was a small fish in the war against terrorism.

The sharks of Al Qaeda and other terror organizations are still swimming free, waiting to pounce.

Article 44
Walking Mom Down the Aisle (Indianapolis Star, Philadelphia Daily News, February 10, 2004)

It's not every day you get to be the "Father of the Bride" at your mother's wedding. But it's something many middle-aged people will get to do in the future due to the active lifestyles that elderly people are now leading. Society had better get used to seeing elderly people engage in many activities that defy stereotypes—including marriage.

Last February, I walked my mother down the aisle and gave her away to her new husband, Jack, in a wedding in Fort Lauderdale. They met while they were residents of the same condominium in Philadelphia and had dated for about a year.

Jack is a very vibrant 85. He swims laps every day, drives and has all of his mental capacities. And my mother (I'm sworn to "Survivor"-style secrecy about her precise age) is energetic, active and has many interests. She likes to travel, goes to shows and concerts and is an avid walker. Like many other seniors, she has become a geezer geek (she has her own computer and uses it frequently).

I was skeptical when I heard that my mother was getting re-married. It's not something that most 41-year-olds hear from their parents. It took a little getting used to.

Why would people bother getting married so late in life? What will they have—15 years together at the most? Why don't they just live together? Perhaps it's a sign of optimism that they plan to continue to live an active life for quite a few more years.

Many older people lose interest in life and simply give up and pack it in, many times due to health problems. In some cases, their options for getting out and doing things are limited because they are physically unable to drive anymore.

While many older people are living the stereotypical life of an infirm elderly person in an assisted-living home, there are an increasing number like my mom and Jack who remain in good health well into their 80s.

The day before the wedding, my mother, Jack and I were sitting in a Florida restaurant having the early-bird special. It was like Jurassic Park—every patron was a senior citizen.

As if she read my mind, my mother said, "We're not all dinosaurs. Older people like to go out and have active lives."

Elderly adults often seek new challenges. Many have computers and surf the Internet. Others travel. More people in their 80s and 90s will be driving, traveling, playing tennis and golf, having sex—and even getting married.

Although the Census Bureau doesn't keep marriage statistics for people over 70, a CBS News report last year said seniors make up the fastest-growing group of online dating service users. Medical breakthroughs have extended our life expectancies. In the U.S., women live to 80 and men live to 74, on average. According to the American Federation for Aging Research, there will be approximately 500,000 people over 100 by the year 2030. The advent of Viagra has extended other things. As life expectancy rises, society needs to look at elderly people in a different light.

This is the happiest I've ever seen my mother. My parents' marriage ended in a bitter divorce when I was 13. Too many times, due to their animosity toward each other, the only dinner conversation we had was between the silverware as we cut into our food.

Now, the affection my mother and Jack show towards each other is apparent—holding hands, cuddling, laughing at each other's jokes. Aside from listening to Neil Diamond and Barbra Streisand as opposed to N'Sync or Eminem, it's as though they are giddy teens. At midlife, I'm getting to see my mother in the warm, caring, loving relationship with a spouse that I'd always hoped for her when I was a child.

Cupid's arrow can strike at any age. We are social creatures. We need love, kindness, intimacy, companionship and a sense of security throughout our lives.

Article 45
Why High Risk Surgery Sometimes Makes Sense
(Philadelphia Inquirer, April 7, 1997)

My grandmother celebrated her 97th birthday this March. That's a pretty good accomplishment, but there are plenty of people who live until their '90s or even older. How many, though, have undergone and survived double-bypass heart surgery at age 95?

Needless to say, she's a very strong woman. And she was fortunate to have doctors who believed in her strength and who weren't forced to assume that this high-risk operation wasn't economically feasible merely because of her age.

It's easy to talk about Medicare cuts or rationed health care when it's in the abstract. But when it's your close relative, you want the doctors to make the decision, not a bunch of health-care bureaucrats insisting on strict treatment guidelines.

My grandmother, Edith Dubin, has lived a good, long life. She was born in Ukraine, near Kiev, and came to America with her parents and six siblings in 1902. Her family barely escaped the slaughters of Jews during the pogroms, as her mother won a German lottery and the proceeds gave the family enough money to leave the country just in time. She came to the United States, saw Halley's Comet in 1910, took a horse-drawn trolley to see John Phillip Sousa in concert every summer at Willow Grove Park, and stood on the steps of the Bellevue-Stratford hotel to see soldiers returning home in a parade after World War I. She married her husband, Leon, in 1923 and they had three children, four grandchildren, and two great-grandchildren.

At 95, my grandmother was self-sufficient and had her own apartment. She had suffered from angina for years; however, it had been getting worse. Still, it was somewhat controllable with medication. Then, in late July 1995, she collapsed.

Her chest pains continued while she remained hospitalized at Albert Einstein, and the tests showed that she had suffered a heart attack. One of her ventricles was 90 percent closed and a second also was severely damaged.

At first she was given three options: (1) Do nothing and live with the pain and be at risk of a massive heart attack; (2) have a single bypass-a lower risk procedure that would not involve stopping the heart and could buy her another year or two, or (3) have a double bypass, which would involve stopping her heart during the operation, but which could give her several more quality years.

For most 95-year olds, open heart surgery would be unthinkable. However, her vital organs were in good shape and her team of doctors was confident she could survive the operation's rigors.

On the day of the operation, I spent five agonizing hours in the hospital waiting room with my mother, two cousins, and an uncle. Our heads jerked up as one every time a doctor or nurse came out of the operating room. Finally, a doctor emerged from the operating room. "Dubin family?" he said. We all leaned forward. "She's doing fine."

For the next few months, it was still touch-and-go, as she endured severe post-operation complications, including gastrointestinal problems, difficulty breathing, and an inability to eat solid food. In time though, she showed flashes of her old self and I knew she would be OK when she told me to get a haircut and tuck in my shirt.

At this point, her prognosis for long-term survival is good and she gets around without a walker. She's still alert and feisty and she can once again look forward to getting a letter from the President congratulating her on her 100th birthday.

How old is too old to undergo open heart surgery? With proposed cuts in Medicare, would the doctors have even performed the operation on my grandmother, given her advanced age? I don't know the answer to either question. But doctors, HMOs, and the families of elderly heart patients can look to my grandmother as a lesson that age alone shouldn't determine whether a person in his or her 90s should have open heart surgery.

Article 46
A Songsmith Celebration—An Often Forgotten
Writer of Some Unforgettable Songs (Al Dubin)
(Philadelphia Inquirer, September 1998)

He wrote the songs that made the whole world sing. But, like most songwriters who aren't named Gershwin, Cole Porter, or Rodgers and Hammerstein, Al Dubin has been forgotten by most people. For those who recognize his name, they are probably unaware that the lyricist for "42nd Street" and several other Depression-era musicals lived over half his life in Philadelphia.

Al Dubin was born in Zurich, Switzerland in 1891. His parents, Simon and Minna, moved to Philadelphia in 1893, where they settled in a home at 325 Pine Street. Simon, a physician, had a practice in his home, but he also served as the Chief of Gynecology at Mt. Sinai Hospital, which is now Albert Einstein Medical Center. Minna was a chemist who worked at the Dupont Chemical Company at 35 th and Grays Ferry Road. In his teenage years, Dubin frequently went to New York to see musical shows and to hang out in Tin Pan Alley. He enrolled at Philadelphia's Northeast M.T. High School, a vocational school, in order to learn a trade to support himself while he was writing and trying to sell lyrics.

In 1909, Dubin was accepted to the Perkiomen Seminary, a prep school. He became captain of the football and track teams and played forward for the basketball team. While there, he penned the school's alma mater. In addition to song, however, Dubin liked to partake in wine and women. He was expelled in 1911 for drinking and missing curfew.

His parents moved to 40th and Girard in 1911, but Al moved into his own small apartment. He had jobs as a singing waiter in a Philadelphia restaurant and worked as a bartender on Race Street. Simultaneously, he was writing lyrics and trying to sell them to a Philadelphia publishing firm.

After his first modest hit, "Twas only an Irishman's Dream," was published in 1916, Dubin was drafted by the Army. He served briefly in France, but received an honorable discharge with help from his father. His father died in 1919, and

Dubin moved to New York in 1921, where he married Helen McClay and had a daughter, Patricia. Seven years later, Dubin, his wife and daughter, and his step-daughter Marie moved to Hollywood.

In 1929, Dubin wrote the words to "Tip Toe Thru the Tulips" for the film "Gold Diggers of Broadway." (He probably turned over in his grave when Tiny Tim made it his signature song 40 years later). From 1929–1930, Dubin and composer Joe Burke wrote songs for 11 Warner Brothers motion pictures. They also wrote the alma mater for Villanova University, where Burke's son was a student.

In 1932, Warner Brothers hired composer Harry Warren and teamed him with Dubin. They proceeded to pen over 60 hit songs in just six years, including "Forty-Second Street," "Shuffle Off to Buffalo," "We're in the Money," "I Only Have Eyes for You," and "Lullaby of Broadway," which won an Academy Award for best song in 1935 from the movie "Gold Diggers of 1935." The film "Forty-Second Street" set the standard and moved the movie musical to new heights. In all, Dubin and Warren collaborated to write the music for 32 films, including "Forty-Second Street," "Gold Diggers of 1933," "Gold Diggers of 1935," and "Go Into Your Dance." Many of their songs soared to number one on the Hit Parade Radio Show. Among the stars who performed their songs were Jimmy Cagney, Ruby Keeler, Dick Powell, Ginger Rogers, Rudy Vallee, and Al Jolson.

After Warner Brothers forced Dubin to collaborate with fellow lyricist Johnny Mercer on the film "Garden of the Moon," Dubin left Hollywood for good in 1938. He returned to Broadway, where he collaborated with composer Jimmy McHugh. Al Dubin died in 1945 from barbiturate poisoning and pneumonia.

Dubin was elected to the Songwriters Hall of Fame. But if you look at the stars as you walk down Hollywood Boulevard, you won't see Al Dubin enshrined there amongst the celluloid heroes. During Warner Brothers 75th Anniversary Celebration this year, you'll see a lot of Bugs Bunny and Yosemite Sam, but you're not likely to see much of Al Dubin.

Perhaps a bigger oversight is that Dubin hasn't been selected for the Philadelphia Walk of Fame in front of the Academy of Music. Most of the Walk of Fame honorees are well-known performers and celebrities, such as Chubby Checker, Ed McMahon, Al Martino, and Stanley Clarke. While Al Dubin doesn't have the name recognition of these stars, his body of work surely would qualify him as a nominee. Joe Burke, the Philadelphia-born composer who worked with Dubin at Warner Brothers, is a Walk of Fame honoree.

Songwriters are the backbone of musicals, whether on Broadway or the big screen. Without songwriters, there would be nothing to sing or dance to. They're usually overlooked and underappreciated by movie producers and studios as well as the public, who love the songs and the artists who perform them but remain indifferent toward the people who created the songs.

So the next time you go to a theatre to see "Forty-Second Street" or rent the video, just remember that before he shuffled off to Broadway and Hollywood, Al Dubin was a Philadelphian.

Article 47
Three Whoops for the Three Stooges (Philadelphia Inquirer, Couples Series, June 21, 1999)

Ask any 12-year-old kid who Martin and Lewis, Laurel and Hardy, and Abbott and Costello were, and you'll probably get a shrug and a "Huh?" But ask him if he knows who the Three Stooges are and he'll likely respond, "Soitenly, toots!"

The Three Stooges are the most enduring and timeless comedy team of the century. Every generation of kids growing up since the 1930s has been weaned on the eye poke, the eye poke block, and the whirling fist to the top of the head.

During the early '90s, Philadelphia hosted several annual Three Stooges Conventions, which featured screenings of old films, sale and display of merchandise (such as "Just Say Moe" T-shirts), guest speakers, including the Stooges' relatives and actors who appeared in Stooges films, and Stooge impersonators. Being named "Larry," I was happy to get a photo taken of me standing between a Moe and a Curly impersonator at one of those conventions. Last year, a convention was held in Los Angeles where several hundred attendees, including Michael Jackson, Jonathan Winters, and director John Landis, engaged in similar activities, plus a tour of Stooge sites in Los Angeles and a pie throwing fight at $35 a head.

Since the Stooges' heirs were granted joint licensing rights after a 1994 lawsuit, there has been an explosion of Stooge merchandising, including rereleased film footage, books, Three Stooges beer, Three Stooges lottery tickets, a cookbook, and lunch pails. During the early '90s, Stooges films appeared regularly on the Family Channel. Columbia TriStar and Comedy III Productions recently made digitally remastered versions of Three Stooges shorts available for syndication and cable television.

The Three Stooges began as a vaudeville act in the 1920s, known as Ted Healy and his Stooges. Samuel Horwitz ("Shemp Howard") was in this original lineup along with Harry Moses Horwitz ("Moe Howard") and Louis Feinberg ("Larry Fine"), but he left the group and was replaced by his brother Jerome Horwitz ("Curly Howard") in 1932. Ted Healy subsequently went on his own, and

Columbia pictures picked up the Stooges. Shemp rejoined the group after Curly suffered a stroke in 1946, and he served as "Third Stooge" until his death in 1955. He was replaced by Joe Besser, who was in turn replaced by Joe DeRita ("Curly Joe"). The Stooges made 190 short subject films with Columbia from 1934 through 1959 and subsequently appeared in several feature length films, including the "Three Stooges Meet Hercules." They also appeared frequently on the Ed Wynn, Frank Sinatra, and Ed Sullivan television shows. In 1958, the Columbia short films were released to television, and the Stooges became even more popular, especially with children who never had seen their prior body of work. Joe DeRita, the last living Stooge, died in 1993.

What made the Stooges so popular and enduring? For one, they helped us get in touch with the "inner Stooge" that exists in all of us. They represented the "common man" and poked fun at rich, snooty, and pretentious people and professions—a very popular theme during the Depression. The Stooges got away with things in their films that most of us would love to do in real life, but can't, due to societal mores. Wouldn't you love to give an eye poke or a triple face slap to some "lame-brain" at the local gym, or twist the nose of a hated "wiseguy" co-worker with a pair of pliers?

The Stooges parodied everyone including doctors ("calling Dr. Howard, Dr. Fine, Dr. Howard"), lawyers (in one episode, they portray the law firm of Dewey, Cheatum, and Howe), dentists (who needs Novocaine when you can use a hammer and chisel?), radio personalities ("Quiet numbskulls, I'm broadcasting"), and the horse racing industry ("She was bred in old Kentucky, but she's just a crumb down here"). They were the first film performers to portray Adolph Hitler in a negative light, at a time when it was controversial to do so.

Whenever I have to make a speech or public appearance, I don't relax myself by picturing the audience in their underwear. I just think of Curly pretending to be a college professor and singing the B-a Bay B-e Bee B-i Bicki B-i song. When I see Niagara Falls on television, I think of water gushing from the television when the boys acted as plumbers in a rich mansion. Whenever I hear the phrase, "The sword of Damocles is hanging over your head," I think of Moe sweating profusely as a blueberry pie dangles over his head during one of the classic pie fights.

The Stooges weren't for everyone. They never caught on big with women, the snooty hoity toity, and other assorted knuckleheads who took themselves too seriously and frowned upon the Stooges' slapstick, physical comedy.

The Stooges also were unappreciated for years by serious film connoisseurs. But noted film critic Leonard Maltin included them in his book, "The Great Movie Comedians."

"Snobbism has excluded them from most "respectable" surveys of screen comedy, but the time has come for at least some rudimentary recognition," says Maltin. "The Three Stooges lasted for more than 40 years because they were funny."

The Three Stooges never won any Oscars. They'll never be confused with comedic groundbreakers like Charlie Chaplin or Woody Allen. Yet, in their own simple way, they were geniuses.

Article 48
Funny-tawkin' Pats Fans Will Be Crying in Their Chowdah (Hartford Courant and Philadelphia Daily News, February 1, 2005)

SORRY ALL you chowderheads, but you New England Patriots fans don't deserve to win the Super Bowl. The Patriots have enjoyed a great deal of success lately, winning two Super Bowls in the past three years. Last year, Boston Red Sox fans got to celebrate their first World Series title since 1918. The only parades Philadelphia fans have had since the 76ers championship in 1983 have been the Mummers'. Now it's our turn.

For many years, New England fans didn't live and die with the Patriots, who were usually the poor stepchild of the Red Sox and Celtics. Boston is known mostly as a baseball town, and unless the Patriots are winning, many Bostonians don't give a hill of beans about the team.

It's only when the Pats became successful recently did the bandwagon form. As reported by the Boston Globe on April 2, 1993, the Patriots had lost millions of dollars due to poor attendance at Foxboro Stadium (the Pats' former home) and an allegedly unfair lease, and they were threatening to move to St. Louis if a new stadium was not built. According to a 1992 St. Louis Post-Dispatch article, the Patriots lost $12 million in 1990 and about $10 million in 1991 due to poor attendance and a bad stadium deal.

When the Patriots were losing back in those days, the fans' nonchalant attitude was something like, "Well, gee, gosh golly—we'll go out and try hahdah next season." When the Eagles lose in the playoffs, fans go into a monthlong depression. While it took the Tom Brady Bunch to rub off on the New England area and finally awaken their long-slumbering fan base, Eagles fans have stuck with their team through thick and thin.

Much has been made over the Curse of the Bambino, broken last fall by the Red Sox when they won their first World Series title since 1918. But spare us the violins for your long Red Sox drought. If you multiply 21 seasons times 4, repre-

114

senting the four major sports of football, baseball, basketball and hockey (remember it?), Philadelphia sports teams have suffered through 84 seasons of zero championships. Some people have dubbed this "The Curse of William Penn," since the championship drought started right after the city dropped its long-standing tradition of not allowing any buildings to stand taller than City Hall. Since 1983, every other city with four major sports teams has won at least one championship.

Over the years, Philadelphia sports fans have done a lot of things to deserve their reputation as a tough crowd—throwing snowballs at Santa Claus, booing the Easter Bunny, throwing batteries at J.D. Drew, booing the selection of Donovan McNabb at the NFL draft, booing Cowboys' receiver Michael Irvin as he was lying motionless on the Vet turf, throwing snowballs at Cowboys coach Jimmy Johnson, brawling in the stands, attacking fans of other teams and urinating in the sinks and the floor at the Vet.

At times, you can question Philly fans' sanity. But you can never question their passion. Even though our teams have broken our hearts throughout the years, including three straight NFC Championship game losses, we keep coming back. Win or lose, we'll fly Eagles flags at home and on cars, and we'll always keep wearing team jerseys and caps.

So no Chunky Soup for you, Patriots fans. Donovan McNabb and the Eagles are going to dish out a beating that will be wicked hard-core (or wicked hahdcaw, as you might say up there). Super Bowl Sunday will be a Green Day for the Eagles and their long-suffering fans. After all, we've had too many years walking down the Boulevard of Broken Dreams.

Article 49
Put 'em in Coach (A Little Leaguer Fires a Shot Heard By Benchwarmers 'Round the World). (Cleveland Plain Dealer, Philadelphia Inquirer, September 3, 1998)

Chris Cardone, the 4-foot-10-inch Little League's version of "Mr. August," didn't just hit the game-winning home run last Saturday for his Toms River, New Jersey, team. He struck a blow for everyone who ever has been a bench-warmer on a youth sports team.

Cardone was good enough to be selected to the Toms River All-Star Team, but he saw limited playing time as a reserve outfielder during the Little League World Series and had gone 1 for 10 in World Series at-bats before the final game. He had hit only one home run during the entire season.

Trying to keep his spirits up even though he wasn't playing much, his mother had told him to be patient and wait his turn. He said, according to the New York Post, "Mommy, there are no 'taking turns' in baseball."

Maybe you were the kid who was stuck in right field watching dandelions grow while your coach and teammates prayed that no one hit the ball to you. Or maybe you were the kid who was good enough to make a varsity team but never got a sniff of playing time.

It's a shame that the passion to win at all costs plays such a big part of youth sports. Many leagues may have rules requiring that the kids play a certain number of innings in a baseball game or certain number of minutes in a basketball game. That trend is good.

But coaches still stick their worst kid in right field and make sure that their best players are on the field or the court at crunch time at the end of the game. Traveling teams and most junior high or junior varsity teams don't have minimum playing requirements. I've heard horror stories of Little League coaches who encouraged the worst players not to show up for playoff games or intentionally told them the wrong time of the game.

116

Many coaches probably think they're doing their deep subs a favor by not playing them because the kids would only screw up and embarrass themselves. But I think the majority of kids are burning inside, saying to themselves, "Come on, coach, give me a shot."

These kids just want the chance to prove themselves. Sometimes they just need experience and playing time to build their confidence. Even if they do screw up, they always can try another sport. Many kids with latent talent quit youth sports altogether because they're never given that shot.

When I was at Cheltenham High School in the late 1970s, I tried out for the junior varsity soccer team in 10th grade. I never had played soccer before and it showed. During my first practice, I was supposed to trap a punt from a goalie, but instead the ball clanked off my head and went 20 feet in the air. My junior varsity days were frustrating, as I gathered serious splinters sitting on the bench. I had a coach who didn't want to play any of his deep subs, even when we were losing 4–0 late in the game, the equivalent of a 75-point lead in the fourth quarter of a basketball game. I think I got to play in about three junior varsity games in two years.

Nonetheless, I worked hard and improved. In my senior year, I played really well during summer tryouts—well enough to make the varsity team. I was thrilled to be selected for the varsity team and I yearned to play. But my playing time was sparse—in only about one-third of the games, mostly during blowouts. I knew that the starters were better than I was, but I just wanted a chance to prove to myself that I could play at this level.

Finally, in our last game of the season, the coach put his senior subs into the game for most of the first half. I more than held my own as a defensive fullback, breaking up many scoring opportunities and getting some steals. I even had a nice run with the ball upfield and had an assist on what seemed like the go-ahead goal. (Unfortunately, this wasn't a Disney movie, as the play was called offsides. It was a bad call.) We ended up in a 1–1 tie.

Even if the coach's move to give us so much time in an important game situation was a token gesture, I felt that I had proved something to myself and was a real part of the team, at least for one day. And I had answered the question that had plagued me for three years. I could play at the varsity level.

From now on, I hope that when youth league and junior high coaches look down the end of their bench toward the end of the game, they won't see Timmy Lupus of the Bad News Bears anymore. Maybe they'll see Chris Cardone instead. Give that kid a shot. Put him in the game. Maybe he'll surprise you. And himself.

Article 50

Hockey Should End the Brawling (Cleveland Plain Dealer, Philadelphia Inquirer, Dallas Morning News, February 3, 1998)

One of the featured sports at this month's Winter Olympics in Nagano, Japan, will be ice hockey. What makes the Olympic ice hockey tournament more interesting than usual is that professional athletes such as Eric Lindros, John LeClair and Peter Forsberg will be allowed to play for their countries.

Another interesting aspect of the tournament is that these professional players will be playing great, entertaining hockey—without dropping their gloves to fight.

Isn't that an oxymoron? A hockey game without a fight? Hopefully, the games will be great and exciting. Perhaps they even will be good enough to convince the National Hockey League that if it ever wants to make it as a truly major sport in this country, it should, like other legitimate major sports, ban fighting.

In parts of the United States where hockey is not played, the sport either is ignored or is considered a joke. Hockey is perceived as WWF on ice. It is the only sport in which the referees step away and let the players duke it out like rock 'em-sock 'em robots. Video of fighting accounts for half of the NHL highlights shown on local TV news in places like, say, Charlottesville, Va., or Boise, Idaho.

I lived in Charlottesville in 1987, the year the Philadelphia Flyers played the Edmonton Oilers in the Stanley Cup finals. I hadn't signed up for cable TV, and I went from bar to bar to try to find the seventh game of the series. After much begging and cajoling, I finally convinced one bar to turn the game on. Needless to say, I was the only person watching the game. People would walk by and snicker as if I was watching QVC, the Food Channel or Australian rules football. Every once in awhile, the waitress would say, in her sarcastic twang, "Hey darlin', who's winnin' the game?" Yeah, like she cared.

Compared to other major sports, the NHL's Nielsen ratings are pathetic. Game 1 of last year's Stanley Cup finals drew a 4.0 rating and last year's NHL All

Star Game drew a 2.8. Game 5 of the Eastern Conference final between the Flyers and the New York Rangers, two high-profile teams in major TV markets, drew a 2.4 rating. In contrast, in Games 3 through 7 of the World Series, the ratings ranged from 15.5 to 24.5. The NCAA Championship basketball game drew an 18.9. Game 4 of the NBA finals drew a 16.9 rating. A recent Monday night football game between San Francisco and Denver drew an 18.0.

Even minor sports events, such as the Indy 500 (6.6), Daytona 500 (8.6), Byron Nelson (4.9) and Colonial Golf tournaments (5.9), World Figure Skating Championships (8.3) and the Preakness (5.0), easily outdraw Stanley Cup finals ratings.

Over the years, many people have criticized the NHL's indifference toward hockey fighting. Last year, Ken Dryden, the former Montreal goalie and current president of the Toronto Maple Leafs, called for a ban on hockey fighting.

"As far as I'm concerned, the NHL should not be treating fighting as though it is part of the game," Dryden told a Canadian newspaper. "In my view, if an NHL player fights, he should be ejected, plain and simple, just as players in baseball or basketball are....Essentially, we've been programmed to consider constant fighting in hockey as if there isn't a choice, as if there is an inevitability to it. Well, I don't think there is."

This is the biggest rationale for hockey fighting—that it is part of the game because of the physical nature of the sport. Yet, you don't see fights in the NFL, even with big, fat, sloppy 325-pound linemen hammering the heck out of each other on every play.

The NBA is strictly against fighting—just look at the recent two-game suspension of the 76ers' Derrick Coleman for his altercation with Corliss Williamson of the Sacramento Kings. If fighting is an integral part of ice hockey, why is it not allowed in the Olympics or in high school and college hockey?

Hockey fighting is not tolerated in the NCAA. If a player has a fight in a game, he is disqualified for that game as well as the next game. If the same player fights again later in the same season, he is disqualified for that game and the next two games. Likewise, fighting is not tolerated in the Olympics. If a player fights during an Olympic game, the International Ice Hockey Federation Rules mandate a minimum one-game suspension, with the possibility of a discipline committee imposing further penalties.

Sure, to many people, fighting makes hockey more entertaining. Then again, nude cheerleaders would spice up the NFL and giant windmills and other obstacles planted on the course would make golf more interesting. If you want to see pro athletes slug it out, watch boxing in Las Vegas or Atlantic City. Buy Evander Holyfield's next fight on pay-per-view. Watch kick-boxing on ESPN.

I'm not saying that the NHL should become as dainty as the Ice Capades. You still can have exciting hockey with hard-hitting checks and digging for the puck in the corners. But the NHL has to ban fighting if it ever wants to be taken seriously as a major sport. Otherwise, it still will be perceived as the Three Stooges on ice. With twice as many eye pokes.

Article 51
Don't Cry for the Big East. (Philadelphia Daily News, Baltimore Sun, July 1, 2003)

Shed no tears for the Big East Conference as it gets plundered by the Atlantic Coast Conference.

Just in case any of you had any delusions that college sports are about purity, fun and honest competition, you're kidding yourselves. It's a cold-hearted, calculating, bottom-line business. For many years, the Big East has specialized in being cold-hearted. What goes around comes around, and in losing its two premier football schools, the University of Miami and Virginia Tech, to the ACC, the Big East is getting what it deserves.

In 2001, the Big East conference made the announcement that it was kicking Temple's football program out of the league. Negotiations pushed the date of Temple's ouster to 2005.

Sure, Temple football was an embarrassment during the 1990s, with a 19–91 record during 10 seasons, a 9–58 record in the Big East and low attendance figures, which bottomed out to around 4,000 fans per game in 1995.

But there had been many signs of life and revival for Temple's program when it got the Big East boot. The Owls had not finished in last place in the Big East since 1996 and just once since 1994. In 2000, Temple had a 4–7 season, its best since 1990. The school recently had built a $7 million on-campus practice facility, and it's scheduled to play at Lincoln Financial Field, the Philadelphia Eagles' new stadium, starting this year. Its home attendance had increased to an average of 18,700 in 2000.

Experts had praised Temple's incoming recruiting class as being its best in years, and, given that Temple was returning all but two of its players from the previous year's team, one Internet poll had Temple ranked in its preseason Top 25 in 2001. Just when Temple football was beginning to show signs of life, the Big East pulled the plug. No warning. No notice. The conference chose to boot Temple despite the existence of pitiful and pathetic Rutgers, which has been an even bigger football doormat than Temple.

For the past two months, the Big East whined about the ACC's attempt to take away Miami, Syracuse and Boston College. No doubt it will whine again as Virginia Tech and Miami depart and Syracuse and Boston College get shafted and left at the altar.

The remaining Big East football schools filed a lawsuit seeking to prevent the ACC's expansion at their expense and alleging that Miami and Boston College promised loyalty to the Big East while planning to depart for the ACC.

Presidents of the Big East universities had asked for a meeting with their ACC counterparts and urged them not to rush to a decision on expansion. During a recent news conference, Big East Commissioner Mike Tranghese whined, "This will be the most disastrous blow to intercollegiate athletics in my lifetime. It's wrong."

The Big East got nine U.S. senators to sign a letter sent to Miami President Donna Shalala urging the universities not to join the ACC since it would have a devastating impact on the Big East's remaining schools.

But the Big East has had no problems in the past pilfering teams from other conferences to join their league. During the past 10 years, it has enticed West Virginia, Rutgers and Virginia Tech to leave the Atlantic 10 in basketball to join the Big East in all sports. And there's no doubt that it will return to its pilfering ways soon. In response to the ACC's attempted expansion, the remaining Big East members have been reported to be planning to raid other conferences to pick up teams such as Louisville, Cincinnati, East Carolina and Marquette from Conference USA and Dayton and Xavier from the Atlantic 10.

And the Big East complains about loyalty? Integrity? Try hypocrisy.

Ironically, Mr. Tranghese hadn't expressed much sympathy for schools and conferences that were left out of the Bowl Championship Series alliance, stating earlier this year (as reported on CBSSportsline.com), "I'm not a socialist....They want access. If I were them, I'd want access and money too. All I said to my schools is, 'I'm not giving them your money.'"

I've always preferred college sports to pro sports because even though college sports has its flaws and scandals, there was a certain purity about seeing kids compete for their school and their fellow students, who rush the field after a big win. But the actions of the ACC now and the Big East in the past confirm that college sports isn't for the students or the players; it's about the greedy, cash hungry institutions that will do anything for a buck.

It looks as though the Big East might become the Big Least at the end of this latest round of musical chairs in conference alliances. It has misbehaved in the past, and now it might get relegated to the children's table of big-time college sports.

Don't feel sorry for their spurned teams; they reaped what they sowed.

Article 52
Skilled Women Can Compete Against Men. (Detroit News, Philadelphia Daily News, December 7, 2003)

The year 2003 will go down as The Year of the Tomboy in sports. Several female golfers have participated in a men's professional tournament, including Annika Sorenstam, Suzy Whaley, Michelle Wie, Laura Davies and Jan Stephenson. In October, Se Ri Pak finished in 10th place in a Korean tour event and became the first woman to make the two-round cut in a men's professional tournament since Babe Zaharias did it in 1945.

During the Thanksgiving weekend, Sorenstam finished in second place in the annual Skins game, ahead of Phil Mickelson and Mark O'Meara. She was the first-day leader and shot a 39-yard eagle out of a bunker on a par-5 hole.

Whether these female golfers made the cut in these tournaments is not vital; the important thing is that they chose to test themselves against better competition and typically held their own under immense pressure and scrutiny.

For the most part, men do not want to compete against women in any serious athletic competition at any level, because it's a no-win situation. If the man wins, hey, he only beat a woman, no big deal. But if he loses, he risks humiliation amongst his male peers. Pity a poor male high school wrestler who gets beat by a girl at the 112 lb weightclass and has to suffer through a year of perpetual wedgies, noogies, and towel slaps from his teammates.

I am now and always have been light years away from ever being good enough to be a professional athlete, but like most guys, I've had an aversion about competing with and against women in sports. The few times that I've seen women waiting to play in pick-up basketball games at my gym or at an outdoor court, I cringe and bite my lip, because I don't want to be on her team and wouldn't want her to be guarding me if I were playing for the other team.

However, there have been a couple exceptions when I didn't mind being on the same team as a girl or playing against a woman. In both cases, they were good enough to compete with the guys.

In high school, I played junior varsity and varsity soccer. When I was on the junior varsity team, there was a girl who not only played on the boys' team, but was a starter. It wasn't a token gesture-she was pretty good, she knew how to play, and the rest of the team accepted her.

I currently play in a fairly competitive over-40 basketball league that also allows a few players under 40 to play. Many guys in the league played for their high school teams, and a few played in college. The players take the game seriously, and we have our share of pushing, shoving, fighting, head butts, and suspensions. A few years ago, there was a woman who played in the league who frankly was in over her head. She tried and hustled, but she just didn't know the game and really couldn't compete. While we admired her guts and courage, most guys didn't want her on their team, and no one wanted the humiliation of being the guy that she was guarding.

However, there now is a woman in her mid 30s playing in the league who is a better than average player in the league. She played for her college basketball team and she knows and plays the game fundamentally just as well, if not better, than most of the guys in the league. The other players just see her as one of the guys (except when she missed a year due to her pregnancy).

There shouldn't be an uproar when women want to test themselves to see how they'll compete against men.

Someday, a female goalie might be good enough to earn a roster spot in the National Hockey League. If they chose to do so, the Williams sisters might win a match or two in a men's tournament.

The experience of female athletes playing in men's professional tournaments won't threaten the existence of women's sports. Most women will be content to compete against other women. However, for those extraordinary and skilled women, Annika and the other women have shown it's OK to give it a shot once in a while against the guys and more than hold their own.

Article 53
The Phillies are Making a Pitch to Lure Inner-City Kids to Baseball (Philadelphia Inquirer, June 24, 1995)

Given the greed and arrogance displayed by both sides during baseball's recent labor unrest, it's easy to be cynical when you hear Phillies' management and players talk about becoming fan-friendly and reaching out to the public.

In one case, however, the Phillies truly are reaching out to people who haven't had much exposure to baseball at all—Inner-city kids.

The Phillies Rookie League Program, established in 1989, consists of baseball leagues for inner-city kids under the age of 12. In its six years of existence, the program has grown from 200 original participants to about 6,000 kids playing in 60 leagues.

In 1993, the Phillies started the Reviving Baseball in the Inner-City leagues (RBI). This program provides youth baseball leagues for inner-city kids from the ages of 13 to 18. RBI has 15 different leagues and 1,500 participants. All of the players in both the RBI and Rookie Leagues come from needy areas, and most are blacks and other minorities.

"The goal is to give as many kids as possible the opportunity to play baseball who otherwise wouldn't have the chance," says Rob Holiday, the manager of fan development for the Phillies. "Most of the areas in which we've started leagues haven't seen baseball for years."

Part of the Phillies' involvement consists of working with the city's Department of Recreation in fixing 60 of the city's baseball fields through weeding and planting grass in the outfields and grooming the dirt in the infields.

Funds used to renovate the fields have been obtained through Coca-Cola's "Homers for America" program, which designates one day a year to donate funds to certain city programs nationwide for every home run hit that day in a major league ballpark. Other sponsors include Mellon PSFS and Peco Energy.

Members of the Phillies, including pitcher Heathcliff Slocumb and outfielder Tony Longmire, have supported the program with their presence. Former Phils slugger Dick Allen, who is now employed by the Phillies, is helping to coach one of the RBI teams.

The Phillies also host an annual youth baseball night in which they give away free tickets and provide bus transportation to about 60 busloads of RBI and Rookie Program players.

"These kids are starting to play, and we want them to learn to appreciate the game," says Holiday. "The kids want to play—it's just a matter of organizing groups of adults to help them do it. We want to give the kids something to do, and hope that they develop their interest in baseball as they get older."

According to Holiday, it is estimated that blacks compose only 2 percent to 3 percent of the fans that attend Phillies games. In contrast, the 76ers' fan base of season ticket holders is about 10 percent black, according to estimates by the 76ers marketing and public relations departments.

As Ken Burns repeatedly pointed out in his Baseball documentary, baseball used to be the sport of choice for black Americans, who played whenever and wherever they could during the first half of this century. Black players barnstormed the country playing four games in one day and traveling all night in old, broken-down buses. The Negro Leagues flourished during the 1930s, drawing huge crowds and producing heroes such as Josh Gibson, Satchel Paige and Buck Leonard as well as great teams such as the Kansas City Monarchs, Pittsburgh Crawfords and Homestead Grays.

Clearly, baseball is being challenged, if not already supplanted, as the national pastime by professional football and basketball. This is especially the case in urban areas where basketball is life.

Unlike the '50s and '60s when the idols and role models were named Mays, Aaron and Robinson, today's kids want to grow up to be the next O'Neal, Jordan and Olajuwon; many of them barely have heard of Ken Griffey Jr., Frank Thomas or Tony Gwynn. Most of the top black athletes opt for scholarships in basketball or football and scoff at baseball as an option.

Is African American apathy toward baseball caused by bitterness toward baseball's ugly history of racism and segregation? There may be an element of truth to that, especially among older people. As for today's kids, however, their indifference is probably more attributable to poor marketing by major league baseball as well as the emergence of other sports and diversions.

As baseball seeks to regain many of the fans that it lost to the strike, it is wise to look at minorities and the inner cities as an untapped market yet to be developed. Exposing these kids to baseball at an early age will reap dividends in the future—not just in grooming a top reservoir of talent, but in developing lifelong fans of a sport that used to be number one in every kid's heart, white or black.

Will these kids' hoop dreams ever be replaced by dreams of grand slams, double steals and executing the hit and run? That remains to be seen. For now, however, the Phillies are at least giving them the chance to dream.

Article 54

Booing is Phila. Tradition, But Use Common Sense (Philadelphia Inquirer, October 13, 1999. A revised version was broadcasted as a commentary for Only a Game on National Public Radio.)

As Eagles quarterback temp Doug Pederson and Cowboys receiver Michael Irvin have learned recently, Philadelphia isn't always the place that loves you back. Philadelphia sports fans have a national reputation for being negative, a reputation that's entirely deserved. While Pittsburgh was once known as the "City of Winners," Philadelphia might as well be the "City of Whiners."

Why are we so negative? Maybe it's because we've been deprived for so long. It's been sixteen years since the 76ers won the NBA title and provided the city's last championship. Of the cities with at least four major teams, Philadelphia has gone the longest without a title.

Fans in other regions of the country have their own distinct characteristics and trademark quirks. Chicago Cub fans throw baseballs back onto the field after opponents hit a home run. Duke University basketball fans bob up and down in unison to rattle the other team. Cleveland Browns fans bark and wave dog bones in the end zone's "dawg pound." Los Angeles Dodger fans leave after the sixth inning to beat the traffic.

So what are Philadelphia fans best known for? Booing. White collar and blue collar Philadelphians alike feel that booing is a birthright…as much a part of Philadelphia as cheesesteaks, hoagies, and the Liberty Bell. It is a rite of passage when a Philadelphia dad takes his son to an Eagles game and they share the common bond of heckling an Eagles quarterback when he overthrows a receiver.

Aside from a boycott, booing is the only avenue that the fans have to express their displeasure at how their team is being run and how the players are performing. A group of Eagles' fans recently upheld this tradition when they went to the NFL Draft and proceeded to boo the Eagles' management for taking quarterback

Donovan McNabb instead of running back Ricky Williams or failing to trade their pick to the New Orleans Saints for a riverboatload of draft picks.

I remember my first exposure to cynical Philadelphia fans. In the early 1970s, my father took me to a Phillies double header at Veterans Stadium. Between games, there was some promotion featuring the Easter Bunny in a hot air balloon. The poor rabbit couldn't get his balloon off the ground and a crowd of over 60,000 booed lustily for over ten minutes. Luckily for the bunny, it was springtime and the fans weren't able to pelt him with snowballs like fans did to Santa Claus during halftime of an Eagles home game in the late 1960s.

Of course, the jeering and ill will has not been reserved to the holiday mascots who have had the misfortune to find themselves on the terrifying playing fields of the City of Brotherly Love. Athletes, as it turns out, usually make better targets. It was one thing to boo Von Hayes, whom many scouts had touted as the next Ted Williams. He played more like Vanessa Williams, so the derision was understandable. But it was another thing entirely to boo Mike Schmidt, the greatest Phillie of all time. Schmidt hit 548 career home runs and is considered to be the greatest third baseman in baseball history. The hometown fans at times were merciless, which prompted Schmidt on one occasion to don a wig and sunglasses in a humorous attempt to diffuse tension during fielding practice.

We even boo our fellow fans. At pro and college basketball games, lucky fans are often invited to shoot a halfcourt shot or a series of three pointers to win prizes. Naturally, the unlucky fan usually doesn't hit the backboard, making him or her yet another unfortunate victim of Philly wrath.

Sometimes, though, people lose sight that opposing players are human beings and not evil cartoon characters or Darth Vader action figures. Shame on the numbskulls who threw batteries at the St. Louis Cardinals' J.D. Drew in August and cheered when a stretcher came out for the seriously-injured Dallas Cowboy Michael Irvin. There's a difference between being a dedicated, loyal, and passionate fan justifiably expressing his or her anger with an unproductive player or inept management with a heartfelt boo, and an idiot who loses all perspective, forgets that it's only a game, and crosses that invisible blue line (Hey, I had to fit hockey somewhere in here) to engage in unsportsmanlike conduct.

They can ban tailgating. They can limit beer sales. They can crack down on fights and flare guns in the stands, and I hope they do. But the first amendment is the first amendment, and they can't take away our right to boo. Let's just use some discretion and common sense when exercising that right.

Article 55
Baseball Strike: Bronx Cheer for Players, Owners (Atlanta Journal-Constitution, Cleveland Plain Dealer, Baltimore Sun, Los Angeles Daily News, August 14, 2002)

Baseball players didn't set a strike date Monday as expected, but they might do so on Friday. I couldn't care less. Baseball lost me as a fan several years ago.

What Major League Baseball had better realize is that the national pastime is past its time: It can't afford another work stoppage. It's too late to get me back, but baseball might still save the next generation of fans.

Growing up as a kid in the late 1960s and early 1970s, I loved baseball. It was my favorite sport. I played catch with my father and with friends in my back yard and played several seasons of Little League. I collected baseball cards—not to sell them on eBay, but because I idolized the players. The bubble gum wasn't bad, either.

My father took me to many games at Veterans Stadium in Philadelphia. He even caught a foul ball that I still have today. Through the years, I saw the Phillies' Mike Schmidt make bare-handed plays to get runners out at first base, Steve Carlton pitch masterful complete games and Willie Stargell of the visiting Pittsburgh Pirates hit a 450-foot home run. I even saw the notorious Philadelphia fans boo the Easter Bunny when his balloon failed to get off the ground during a promotion between games of a Phillies doubleheader.

Baseball was king in my neighborhood, and in most neighborhoods in the country at that time.

Throughout the first half of the 20th century, baseball enjoyed a virtual monopoly when it came to professional spectator sports. Pro football didn't become popular until the 1960s; pro basketball became big in the 1980s, and pro hockey saw its popularity increase in the 1990s.

Greed has been good for the players and owners. Today's 850 active Major League players each make more than $2.3 million a year, or nearly $15,000 a game. In December 2000, shortstop Alex Rodriguez signed a 10-year, $252 million deal with the Texas Rangers. Major League franchises are worth nearly $1 billion (the Boston Red Sox recently sold for nearly $700 million). However, there are signs that baseball's popularity is in decline.

There is too much competition for the entertainment dollar for baseball to continue its arrogance. NFL football games sell out and draw large television ratings starting in September. Basketball and hockey playoffs start in April and run until June. That leaves only two months—July and August—in which baseball doesn't face any stiff competition from other sports.

More kids play youth soccer than Little League baseball.

Most die-hard baseball fans are elderly. Every day, hundreds of baseball fans pass on and won't be replaced.

The sad thing about baseball is that its most compelling element is its history.

I haven't watched a complete pro baseball game for about two years. I would almost rather watch QVC or a Bob Saget sitcom rerun. The game's just too slow, and the aloof attitude of most of the millionaire players has turned me away.

It seems as though the players and owners didn't learn anything from 1994's 232-day strike, which resulted in the cancellation of the World Series for the first time in 90 years. Major League Baseball suffered a large drop in attendance in the years following that strike. This year, as of Aug. 1, the average per-game attendance has fallen 5 percent—a loss of 1,533 fans a game.

You need only look to Philadelphia to see the growing apathy toward baseball. In response to the Phillies' consistent failures and numerous last-place finishes over the last 17 years, Veterans Stadium is consistently only one-third full. Attendance is artificially inflated by fireworks nights and give-away days.

Despite the building of new ballparks in Detroit, Chicago and Pittsburgh, attendance in those cities has been disappointing.

Last month, 40 baseball Hall of Famers asked the game's owners and players to use a mediator to settle their work dispute. It seems unlikely that their plea will be answered.

The days of waxing poetic about the joys of baseball are over. Our nation turns its lonely eyes to Kobe Bryant and Kurt Warner, not Joe DiMaggio. We can live without baseball—I've done it for the past seven years. But baseball's owners and players have to realize that they can't live without us, the fans.

Article 56
Sorry, Golf is not a Sport (Chicago Tribune, April 19, 2002). Revised versions of this article were published in the Baltimore Sun and Philadelphia Daily News)

No doubt about it. Tiger Woods' feat of winning his third Masters tournament and seventh major professional golf championship was a great achievement. However, it's a big mistake to compare his feats to other sports.

Last year, many commentators compared the "Tiger Slam" (Woods' winning four straight majors) to other great feats in sports such as Joe DiMaggio's 56-game hitting streak, Wilt Chamberlain scoring 100 points in one game, and Carl Lewis' Olympic feats. Many writers have said that Woods should be considered among the greatest athletes of all time, along with Muhammad Ali, Babe Ruth and Michael Jordan. Some claim that golf is the most difficult sport to master because athletes from other sports try to play it and fail miserably.

Get a grip. Gimme a break.

Woods may be well on his way to being the greatest golfer ever. But it's golf. Golf isn't a sport; it's a skill much like bowling, billiards, darts, auto racing, curling, shuffleboard and pinochle. It's an activity that older people take up when their knees go bad and they can't play real sports like basketball, baseball and football anymore. Sorry, but real sports involve running and jumping. For the most part, pro golfers are a bunch of non-athletes who probably got cut from their high school football and basketball teams and didn't succeed at other sports. How fast would rotund golfers like John Daly or Craig Stadler run a 100-yard dash?

Many golfers in their 40s and 50s are competitive on the pro tour. Mark O'Meara won two major tournaments in 1998 at age 41. Three golfers over age 40 won the U.S. Open during the 1990s. Other well-known over-40 golf geezers who are still competitive on the tour include Greg Norman, Bernhard Langer and Nick Price. One golfer on the Seniors Tour, Larry Laoretti, plays his rounds of golf while smoking a foot-long cigar.

When Casey Martin brought his lawsuit last year asking that he be able to use a golf cart because of a disability, many golfers argued that golf was an athletic endeavor and that walking was an essential part of the sport. Aside from their insensitivity to Martin's degenerative disease in his leg, the golf establishment looked foolish in defending the sport. If walking is a sport, maybe they should give 1st place medals to those who finish first in the Easter Day parade.

Pro golfers take themselves and their sport way too seriously.

They go ballistic if someone dares to take a photograph of them right before they're about to take a shot. Talking on the course? Forget about it. When someone is about to take a shot, the course becomes as silent as a library. Sure, golf takes concentration, but so does taking a foul shot in basketball. You don't see cheerleaders telling the home crowd to be quiet when someone from the visiting team is at the foul line.

Golf should build giant windmills and clown mouths on the course to spice the game up and make it more interesting. Let the golfers play defense on certain holes. Allow fans to heckle and try to distract the golfers when they're about to take a shot. Establish a shot clock mandating that the golfers take their strokes within 35 seconds. Let scantily clad cheerleaders surround the bunkers. Free ice cream for the gallery if a golfer gets a hole-in-one.

Tiger Woods deserves praise for his accomplishments, but put it in perspective. He might have mastered his sport, but if the sports landscape were a Thanksgiving meal, golf would be at the children's table.

Article 57
Athletes Match Up With Student Body (Baltimore Sun, Indianapolis Star, March 27, 2002)

They call the NCAA men's basketball tournament "March Madness," but many people are angry about the perceived failure of student athletes in the classroom.

Critics of the NCAA and student athletes are quick to point to low graduation rates for athletes, but they overlook something: On the average, these athletes are competitive with their peers in the regular student body when it comes to graduation rates.

At face value, the statistics appear to be grim when it comes to student athletes and graduation rates.

ESPN's Outside the Lines has reported that 36 NCAA Division I schools graduated zero percent of their African-American athletes from 1990 to 1994, although they had six years to earn a degree. These schools included Arkansas, Louisville, Cincinnati and Georgia Tech.

The most recent statistics indicate that the graduation rate is 34 percent for Division I basketball players and 48 percent for football players.

The Knight Commission, a panel of university presidents, conference commissioners and athletic officials, recently recommended that if a school failed to graduate 50 percent of its athletes, it should be banned from postseason play.

But NCAA statistics make no distinction between players who drop out for academic reasons, leave school for the National Basketball Association or transfer to another school and receive a degree; all count as non-graduates. Also, the statistics can fluctuate. Since the 1995–96 school year, 81 percent of Georgia Tech's basketball players have graduated or played in the NBA, according to The Atlanta Journal-Constitution.

These statistics also don't reflect the surprisingly low graduation rates for college students nationwide.

The national average for a six-year graduation rate for all students is 55.6 percent. Less than 50 percent of public university students finish school within six years. In 1999, 31 percent of Arkansas college students graduated in five years, well below the national rate of 42 percent for that year. No public university in Pennsylvania graduated more than 40 percent of the freshmen who were admitted in 1997.

According to the most recent NCAA statistics, 35 percent of black male basketball players who entered college in 1994 earned their degrees as compared with 31 percent of the black male student body.

Students, alumni and boosters aren't content with high graduation rates when their teams founder in mediocrity. Notre Dame football coach Bob Davies was fired even though his team had a high graduation rate, because he didn't win a national championship or go to enough major bowl games. It's hard to take seriously the Rev. Theodore Hesburgh, Notre Dame's president emeritus and Knight Commission co-chairman, when he said, "We're not in the entertainment business, nor are we a minor league for professional sports."

Things would improve if the NBA would set up an extensive viable minor league system similar to Minor League Baseball. The NBA recently established an eight-team developmental league, but it has a minimum age limit of 20 (or 18 if a player was drafted and cut by an NBA team). If the NBA were to drop the minimum and expand the number of teams, the developmental league could be similar to baseball's minors. Instead of opting for college, high school student athletes could go straight to the minors.

Student athletes would benefit academically if the NCAA shortened the length of the seasons and practice time. Practice for Division I basketball starts on Oct. 15 and the championship game is played in early April. That leaves up to three months of the school year in which basketball players don't have practice or games. Given the season's length and the substantial amount of time spent on traveling for games and practices, there's little time for athletes to study.

While colleges should try to improve graduation rates for their athletes, as well as all of their students, we shouldn't overhaul the current system because of a few bad apple schools and coaches. When you compare the graduation rates of NCAA Division I athletes and the rest of the student body nationwide, there isn't a major difference. There's room for improvement, but that goes for everyone, not just the student athletes.

Article 58
March Madness, Reputation Destroyer (How one game in the NCAA basketball tournament can determine a coach's reputation forever). (Philadelphia Daily News, March 15, 2004)

MARCH MADNESS is upon us—and it's going to be awesome, baybee. New stars will be born and more than one shining moment will occur. One bounce of the ball, one slip and fall, and one shot can make a legend or create a scapegoat.

No moment is more indicative as to how one play can create an image more than the Houston-North Carolina State NCAA championship game, 21 years ago in Albuquerque, N.M.

The game's last play is part of college basketball lore. As time ran down, an N.C. State pass was nearly stolen by Houston's Benny Anders near midcourt. N.C. State's Dereck Whittenburg hoisted up a desperation 40-foot shot, which was slammed home in the game's last second by Lorenzo Charles, as Houston's Akeem (now spelled Hakeem) Olajawon watched helplessly.

N.C. State's Jim Valvano ran onto the court, frantically looking for someone to hug; Houston's coach Guy Lewis slinked off the court, crying into his trademark red and white polka dot towel, looking for answers.

Valvano became a coaching legend and a national personality. He went on to be a national TV commentator before his untimely death from cancer in 1993 at 47. He is forever remembered for his emotional "Don't ever give up" speech at the ESPY awards.

Guy Lewis, whose team was heavily favored against N.C. State, has become a forgotten figure in basketball history.

Lewis, now 83, had a record of 592 wins and 279 losses in what should be considered a storied career. Since Lewis left, Houston's record as of last week was 259 wins and 265 losses. In the 1983 NCAA semifinal, Lewis' "Phi Slama Jama" team beat Louisville's "Doctors of Dunk," in a memorable dunk-filled game that Houston won 94–81. Lewis coached Houston from 1957 to 1986. He won 31 or more games three times. His teams won two Southwest conference champion-ships, four conference postseason titles, reached 14 NCAA tournaments, and went to the Final Four five times. In the Final Four, Houston lost twice to Lew Alcindor (now Kareem Abdul-Jabbar) and UCLA, once to Michael Jordan and James Worthy's North Carolina, and once to Patrick Ewing's Georgetown. Twenty-nine Lewis players were drafted by the NBA and three—Elvin Hayes, Clyde Drexler and Olajuwon—were voted the NBA's top 50 players of all time. Despite his incredible accomplishments, Lewis is not in the Basketball Hall of Fame.

Expectations weren't astronomical for Houston going into the 1982–83 season. Although they had reached the Final Four the year before, they had lost their leading scorer, guard Rob Williams, who was a first-round NBA draft pick. As a freshman, Olajawon had shown promise, but there was little indication that he was about to become a dominating center.

THE PRESEASON favorites for the '82-'83 season included North Carolina with Jordan, Georgetown with Ewing, and Virginia with Ralph Sampson.

Some of college basketball's greatest coaching legends benefited from a lucky break. North Carolina's Dean Smith won two national championships with the benefit of two fluke plays—Michigan's Chris Webber's calling timeout when his team didn't have any left, and Georgetown's Freddie Brown throwing the ball to James Worthy. If not for those two plays, Smith's legendary status would have been tarnished. Duke's Mike Krzyzewski benefited from Christian Laettner's miracle shot at the buzzer against Kentucky in the 1993 NCAA regional final.

It's a shame that Lewis' great career will always be judged by that one game against North Carolina State.

But that's the nature of the NCAA tournament, where the best team doesn't always win, and one bad game means the end of your season and can define your career.

Article 59

The Day She Was a Better Man (Billie Jean King vs. Bobby Riggs) (Philadelphia Inquirer, Couples series, 1999)

Who is the most significant sports couple of the century? Ruth and Gehrig? Sosa-McGwire? Jordan-Pippen? Ali-Frazier? Wilt-Bill Russell?

Try none of the above.

Try the "libber" vs. the "lobber." In September 1973, Billie Jean King and Bobby Riggs played a tennis match that changed the course of sports and society in the latter part of the 20th century. The event was to women's sports and society's view of women as Jackie Robinson's breaking of the color barrier in baseball was to race relations and civil rights.

A world-class huckster, showman, and self-promoter, Bobby Riggs was a world-class tennis player during the late 1930s and 1940s, winning Wimbledon and three U.S. Open titles. During the early 1970s, he was a loud critic of women's sports, particularly tennis. Riggs was the proud poster boy for the male chauvinist pig who espoused the Archie Bunker mentality that a woman's place was in the bedroom or the kitchen—certainly not on an athletic field. "If a woman wants to get in the headlines," Riggs said, "she should have quintuplets." In May 1973, Riggs challenged and humiliated Margaret Court, who was then the number-one ranked female tennis player in the world, 6–2, 6–1.

But Riggs wasn't finished. The one woman he really wanted to beat was Billie Jean King, and she accepted his challenge. Riggs reportedly hyped his match with King by practicing in a "men's liberation" T-shirt and declaring, "If I am to be a chauvinist pig, I want to be the number one pig."

The "Battle of the Sexes" took place at the Houston Astrodome in front of 30,000 people and a huge nationwide television audience of over 50 million. It was as big an event as the OJ Simpson trial, MonicaGate, or an Evel Knievel jump, with the two participants playing for $100,000, winner-take-all. The match captured the country's attention and had the ambience of a heavyweight title-boxing match. Four college football players dressed as toga-clad slaves carried King onto the Astrodome court on a feathered Egyptian litter. Riggs made his entrance on a Chinese rickshaw hauled by "Bobby's Bosom Buddies,"—a bunch of sexy young women in tight outfits.

The 29-year-old King gave Riggs the equivalent of a sports wedgie, whipping the 55-year old former champion 6–4, 6–3, 6–3. Even though King won 39 Grand Slam tennis titles during her career, including six Wimbledon and four U.S.Open titles, this was easily the biggest win of her life.

King's victory was a clarion call to young girls who wanted to participate in sports. Before the 1970s, women's sports were a tiny blip on the radar screen. Little League and youth sports were for boys only, and girls who dared to be athletic and play sports were tomboys or outcasts.

After King's win, it became socially acceptable and cool for girls to go to tennis courts and work on their groundstrokes instead of their tans, enroll in swimming or gymnastics classes, earn black belts in karate, and swish a 15-foot jump shot. It literally became "I am woman, hear me roar!" in soccer cleats.

The past 25 years have seen a boom in women's sports. Soccer moms and dads now serve as chauffeurs to just as many girls' games as boys. Surveys conducted by the National Federation of State High School Associations indicate that the number of girls participating in high school sports have risen from 294,015 in 1971 to nearly 2.5 million in 1996–1997. Gender equity through Title IX legislation has led to increased spending and visibility for women's college athletics. Women's pro tennis is as popular, if not more, than men's tennis. The women's Final Four is now televised, and the WNBA is drawing big crowds during the summer. Perhaps the crowning moment of women's sports occurred at the 1996 Summer Olympics, where the women's Dream Team stole the spotlight from the uninspired men's basketball team and the women's soccer and softball teams earned prime time coverage en route to gold medals.

King's victory also had a profound effect on how men perceived women. Boys growing up in the '70s and 80's were the first generation to perceive women not just as June Cleaver homemaker types, but as strong, independent, capable people who didn't have to rely on men to provide for their needs. A great deal of that respect evolved from boys competing against girls at the youth sports level and then in high school practicing on adjacent fields. Young men not only started accepting women as athletes, but also as college students, doctors, lawyers, and (gulp!) bosses.

Today, most young female athletes probably haven't heard of Billie Jean King. They definitely wouldn't have heard of Bobby Riggs. But the two of them helped change society's view of women forever.

After Riggs died from cancer in 1995, King wrote in Sports Illustrated, "Bobby Riggs was my friend. I know some people may be surprised to hear that, but he was. The Battle of the Sexes irrevocably bonded us."

Article 60
College Athletes Deserve Much Better (Allowing College athletes to work) (Dallas Morning News, Philadelphia Inquirer, Indianapolis Star, January 6, 1996)

Everyone in big-time college athletics is raking in the dough. That is, everyone except the athletes themselves, who can't even earn money during the school year.

That may be about to change. At the National Collegiate Athletic Association convention in Dallas this week and next, members will vote on whether to allow Division I scholarship athletes to work in the off-season. One proposal caps an athlete's earnings at $1,500 a year.

True, it is hard to think of star college athletes as exploited. Many get the benefit of a full scholarship, free lodging and books, free meals, the chance to wave to Mom on national television and the perks of being a Big Man On Campus.

Still, former NCAA President Walter Byers, in his recent book, Unsportsmanlike Conduct: Exploiting College Athletics, advocates an athletes' bill of rights, which would include abolishing the rule against jobs.

'Athletes should be entitled to the freedoms that are available to other students at the university in such matters as work opportunities, the right to transfer between schools and the right to use their name and reputation for financial gain," he writes.

Some people argue that the notion of 'amateur" college athletics has become a farce and that colleges and universities simply should pay their athletes as "semi-professionals" and not make them attend class. That idea is wrongheaded.

Athletes should be encouraged to get their degrees and not rely on a false hope of turning pro. Only a minuscule number of the thousands of young men who play Division I football and basketball ever reach the promised land of pro sports.

But athletes should have a chance to hold jobs and earn spending money, as their fellow students do. And the amount shouldn't be limited to $1,500. Similarly, they should be able to market themselves and promote products, as their coaches can.

If Villanova basketball coach Steve Lappas can make $75,000 from his shoe contract, why can't his star player, Kerry Kittles, be paid to appear at an autograph show or do a television commercial for a sporting goods store?

And if a player has the ability, he ought to be allowed to write columns for local newspapers or publish a diary describing his experiences during the season.

The NCAA's justification for the ban on employment is that it would be hard to monitor legitimate employment arrangements and that the athletes should focus on academics during the off-season and not have the added stress of holding a job.

But there is nothing corrupt about allowing someone to earn money through hard work. It would diminish the athletes' temptation to accept illicit funds from unscrupulous boosters or from gamblers trying to influence a point spread.

You don't have to make athletes employees or give them a huge slice of the NCAA revenue pie. But it is hypocritical to let the coaches and the schools gorge themselves like pigs, while the athletes can't even scramble for the crumbs.

Article 61
Will Phillies Ever Enjoy Another Dream Season?
(Philadelphia Inquirer, April 3, 1993)

Where were you in October, 1980 when the Phillies won the World Series?

I was in my dorm room at La Salle University watching with 10 others as Tug McGraw struck out Willie Wilson. We piled out to Olney Avenue where hundreds gathered to celebrate. A large group of us proceeded to pound repeatedly on a SEPTA bus until La Salle's president, Brother Patrick Ellis, ordered us to stop. Undaunted, we marched our way up to Broad Street where thousands of people of all walks of life gathered to yell, drink and rock parked cars back and forth.

Alas, 13 years have passed and my interest in baseball has diminished. For a while I thought it was the high salaries, pampered athletes, World Series games ending at 1:00 a.m. and the slowness of the game. However, upon further reflection, I've come to realize that my diminished interest in baseball corresponded with the demise of the Phillies.

There hasn't been a meaningful baseball game played in this city in August or September since 1983. The Phillies have finished in last place three of the last six years and have not had a winning season since 1986. Yet every spring, the overly optimistic Phillies' brass tells us what a great team they have if they stay healthy, and the Phillies' fans buy it. Despite the team's recent lack of success, attendance has remained strong as the team consistently draws approximately two million fans a year.

This past winter, the Phillies had a golden opportunity to make some bold moves by signing high-profile free agents. But instead of getting superstars such as Barry Bonds, Kirby Puckett, Ruben Sierra, David Cone and Greg Maddux, the Phillies settled for bargain-basement players such as Milt Thompson, Pete Incaviglia and Danny Jackson. The fans were looking for a home run and we got a bunt single instead.

The Phillies clearly have gone against the message sent by general manager Lee Thomas who said last summer, "What we need right now is a genuine No. 1

starter. Bill (Giles) made the statement that he's willing to go out and try to get somebody." Upon the signing of Danny Jackson, who has won only 21 games since 1988, Thomas said, "At the time we thought we were going to be able to spend a lot more money than we feel we can do now...If there's any fans or anybody out there that would want to do it different and dig into their own pockets, let 'em do it."

Obviously, as the New York Yankees, Los Angeles Dodgers and New York Mets have proven recently, you don't automatically win pennants by merely throwing out money and buying free agents. However, since 1980, the Phillies have signed just one high-profile free agent, Lance Parrish, admittedly a flop. Phillies fans aren't necessarily looking for a pennant winner; they're simply looking for a competitive team with a hopeful future and for a good-faith effort by Phillies' management to produce a winner. Fiscal sanity is one thing, but for a team in the nation's fourth largest media market to have the 17th largest payroll in baseball (as of the beginning of this season) is not putting forth a good-faith effort.

Look at the Flyers. They haven't made the playoffs for three years. However, by making the effort to go out and spend the money for a bona fide superstar, Eric Lindros, they deflected a lot of growing unrest and apathy. Most local hockey fans won't be that upset if the Flyers don't make the playoffs again this year; they see hope in that they have a young team bolstered by Lindros as its cornerstone for the next ten years.

Right now the Phillies have no bona superstars. While Lenny Dykstra, John Kruk and Darren Daulton are good players and have appeared in All-Star games, the Phillies have no perennial all-stars and no one on the current roster, except perhaps Dale Murphy, is likely to be a threat to gain many Hall of Fame votes. Likewise, there are too many "ifs" in a pitching staff that had the National League's worst ERA in 1992. Their farm system is in decline and has been consistently rated one of the worst in baseball.

In his inaugural address, President Clinton exclaimed that we, the voters, had "forced the spring"-a time of renewal and hope. He also spoke of how Americans would have to sacrifice in order to turn things around. These themes can be applied to this year's Phillies. Instead of being forced to watch the Phillies this spring, we can force a new spring by not going out to support the team. Go visit Camden Yards in Baltimore to watch the Orioles play or go watch minor league baseball in Reading or Scranton; heck, you can mow the lawn, take the kids to the Franklin Institute, go to the shore, or even watch your tape of the Eagles-Cowboys Monday night game.

By sacrificing one year of Philllies' baseball, we can get the message out to Bill Giles and the consortium of owners he answers to that we're fed up with the product they're giving us and they're going to have to stop taking the fans for granted.

Perhaps I'm being too pessimistic. Yes, it's true that the rest of the teams in the Eastern Division have gotten worse because the Cubs and Expos have lost key players. I really want the Phillies to do well. It would put the magic back in baseball and give the sports fans in this city a needed boost. It's just that in recent years we've all been promised a Field of Dreams and in turn have received a season of nightmares.

Article 62
He was wrong to boo the Phils; now he wants Braves tomahawked (Philadelphia Inquirer, October 1993)

Okay. This will be painful, but it's time to 'fess up-I was wrong about the Phillies. Boy was I wrong.

I wrote an op-ed piece ("Will the Phillies ever enjoy another dream season?" on April 3) that lamented how my interest in baseball had diminished due to the dismal state of the Phillies. The Phloundering Phillies hadn't fielded a winning season since 1986.

I criticized a team, with only the 17th largest payroll in baseball, for failing to sign high-profile free agents and settling for "bargain-basement" players such as Milt Thompson, Pete Incaviglia and Danny Jackson. And I didn't stop there. I urged fans to sacrifice one year of Phillies baseball to give the Phils' management the message that we were fed up with the product they were giving us. Yes, I wanted to Phils to do well and bring the magic back in baseball here, but I was tired of the overly optimistic Phillies brass annually promising a Field of Dreams, but delivering seasons of nightmares in return.

I wasn't alone in my criticism. When Incaviglia was signed, the Daily News headline the next day proclaimed, "Inky? For Pete's Sake." When the Phils acquired Danny Jackson, Inquirer columnist Frank Dolson questioned the Phils' failure to live up to their promise to go after a topnotch pitcher. (Just how many games did that David Cone win this year?)

Inquirer baseball writer Frank Fitzpatrick called the Phils' winter signings disappointing and said many longstanding fans and several players were frustrated that management wasn't spending money for a star or two.

Other assorted local media types ripped Phils' management and picked them to finish behind the Cubs, the Mets and/or the Marlins. Scores of furious fans barraged the sports call-in shows ridiculing the Phils' acquisitions and vowing not to renew their season tickets.

The national media weren't much kinder to our beleaguered Phils. Baseball Digest picked the Phils to finish fifth in the National League East and Sports

Illustrated's baseball preview had them sixth. Street and Smith's baseball preview even had the audacity to pick the Mets-the Mets?-to win the East and to pick the Phils last behind the expansion Marlins.

Admit it. In March, when Frank Dolson and the Daily News' Bill Conlin picked the Phils to finish first, didn't their foolish picks make you whether Beavis and ButtHead had managed to tap into their computer terminals?

So what happens? The worst-to-first Phillies make a miracle. Milt Thompson leaps over a fence in San Diego to rob the Padres of a homerun; Danny Jackson remembers how to pitch; Inky hammers 24 homers, for Pete's sake, and a kid named Kevin Stocker fields like the reincarnation of Larry Bowa and hits over .300.

The Phils end up winning 97 games—more than the 1980 World Champs and the 1983 National League champs. Every one of the starting pitchers wins in double figures. Lenny Dykstra leads the league in runs, hits and walks and makes a strong run for MVP. John Kruk, the epitome of this tough, fun-loving, and well-fed team, does a guest spot on David Letterman and displays a comic timing right up there with his hitting prowess.

Sure, it's usually nice to look back on a correct prediction and say, "I told you so." In this case, it's better to be wrong—to see the folks in the city—bandwagon jumpers and diehard fans alike—so excited about baseball again.

Fans are the lifeblood of professional sports. We pay our money and that gives us the right to put in our two-cents worth—in Philly, it means we have the right to boo the players when they don't perform and criticize the front office when it's derelict. I still believe it's OK to encourage others to stay away from the park to send a team's management a message.

But this time I wrong to be Doubting Thomas (Phils general manager Lee Thomas, that is.) Maybe I could atone for my sin by making a positive suggestion for the playoffs.

Remember back in the 1977 League Championship Series when Phils fans rattled Dodgers pitcher Burt Hooten by cheering wildly whenever he got behind on the count? Why don't we do the same thing to the Braves' pitchers? Whenever a Braves' pitcher gets to 2–0 on a batter, let's stand up, cheer, and stomp our feet.

As for me, I'll be rooting for our Phighting Phils to tomahawk-chop those Braves. But instead of ballpark hot dogs, I'll be chewing on crow.

Article 63
How Soccer Can Keep The Eagles in Philly
(Philadelphia Inquirer, October 12, 1996)

Are you ready for some soccer—entertaining, hard-fought and pretty skillful American-style soccer? If you haven't already watched a Major League Soccer (MLS) match on TV this season, you've missed a treat. And it's not too late—the playoffs are in full swing, with the championship game scheduled for Oct. 20.

Since the first game in April, the caliber of play in the new league has consistently improved, drawing good (and enthusiastic) crowds, especially in cities such as New York, Los Angeles, and Washington.

Go ahead, local soccer bashers. Keep on ignoring the sport that enjoys tremendous popularity among younger Americans. But if you want the Eagles to stay in Philadelphia, it might help to pretend to be soccer fans. At least for a while.

In Philadelphia, there is a debate about whether the city should build a baseball stadium, a football stadium, or both. Those who argue that a football-only stadium is impractical point out that such a facility would be a waste because it would be used only 10 times a year for Eagles regular season and preseason home games. Eagles' owner Jeffrey Lurie has recognized this and has looked into the possibility of an MLS franchise here.

Major League Soccer's regular season runs from April through September, with each of the league's 10 teams playing 16 of its 32 games at home. The league has major corporate sponsors and a good television package with ESPN, ABC, and the Spanish-language Univision.

Philadelphia's original attempt to land an MLS franchise was unsuccessful because it did not have a suitable grass field stadium as required by the league. If a football stadium were built there, it could play host to MLS games during the spring and summer.

True, Major League Soccer might be a disaster or drown in a sea of apathy. Then again, it might not. America got swept up in World Cup fever in 1994, with large crowds and very solid television ratings that shocked soccer bashers.

This year, the Los Angeles Galaxy drew more than 69,000 fans in their MLS debut at the Rose Bowl (no, it's not true that 68,000 consisted of women who were there just to see Melrose Place star Andrew Shue play for the Galaxy).

The league's teams have averaged close to 17,000 in attendance through mid-September. As of that date, Los Angeles was averaging 29,000 fans per game, significantly higher than the average attendance of such baseball teams as the Phillies and the Mets.

While Joe on the Mobile Phone may never call up the local sports talk shows to talk about whom he likes in the MLS playoffs, legions of soccer-playing kids are yearning for role models and would likely drag their kicking-and-screaming parents to the games.

If the league were to market itself to this young audience, it might be able to carve itself a niche of loyal fans as the NHL has done. Then again, a better analogy might be the Philadelphia Wings, who, despite the absence of media coverage, manage to draw near sellout crowds at the Spectrum for indoor lacrosse. This winter, an indoor soccer team, the Kixx, will try to achieve similar support.

And even without a nice new stadium with a grass field, the A-league—the top minor league—is looking at putting a franchise in Bucks County. While it would be delusional to think that soccer games in Philadelphia would consistently sell out a 60,000-seat stadium, and average of 20,000 fans per game might be achievable.

It's at least worth thinking about. If the MLS defies the odds and does succeed as a major sport, it could help justify the building of a football stadium that wouldn't grow weeds during the off-season.

Article 64
When B-Ball Was the Promised Land (Tamir Goodman and Jewish basketball).(Philadelphia Daily News, January 2002). Revised versions of this article appeared in the Baltimore Sun, Philadelphia Inquirer, B'nai B'rith Jewish Monthly, and as a commentary for Only a Game on National Public Radio)

Oy! Vay! This guy can play.

That's what basketball experts around the country have said about the "Jewish Jordan," Tamir Goodman, an observant Orthodox Jew who made his college basketball debut last season for Towson University in Maryland. Goodman, who averaged 25 points and 9 assists per game for Takoma Academy in his senior year of high school, was selected co-Most Valuable Player for the Capital All-Stars in the Capital Classic.

The University of Maryland offered Goodman a basketball scholarship in January 1999, but he subsequently rejected the offer, stating that the Maryland coaching staff was uncomfortable with his refusal to play on the Sabbath. He has been profiled in Sports Illustrated and on "60 Minutes," as well as many other media outlets.

While Goodman, who might be more like the Jewish Eric Snow than the Jewish Michael Jordan, didn't exactly set the college basketball world on fire last year, he wasn't chopped liver either. He quickly broke into Towson's starting lineup as a Freshman and averaged 6 points and nearly 4 assists for the season. He is the only player in Division 1 basketball to wear a yarmulke during a game, and he has become a celebrity and a role model to Jews across the country. At Towson's game at Long Island University in early December, about one-third of the crowd of 675 were wearing yarmulkes and had come specifically to see Goodman play. He missed the entire first half of one of Towson's America East Conference tournament games because it was played on a Saturday night. Goodman, who scored 13 points and had 6 assists against Big East power Villanova, and had a season-high 16 points against Liberty University, also is going against the grain of a misleading stereotype regarding Jews and sports, particularly basketball.

To most people today, Jewish basketball is an oxymoron right up there with jumbo shrimp and veggie burgers. When they think of Jewish basketball, they may picture old fat guys named Shecky and Moe hoisting two-handed set shots at the local gym. After all, don't Jewish kids have Chicken Soup Dreams, not Hoop Dreams? But, people forget that 60 or 70 years ago, basketball was important in the lives of young Jews at least for those in the cities who played the game incessantly.

As described in a 1992 book by Peter Levine, "Ellis Island to Ebbets Field: Sport and the American Jewish Experience," around the turn of the century there was a popular view of Jews as being inferior, physically incompetent, and repulsed by athletics. Children of Jewish immigrants turned to sports to challenge these stereotypes. Both as spectators and as participants, Jewish involvement in basketball, especially between 1900 and 1950, was greater than in any other sport. By the late 1930s, sportswriters described basketball as the "Jewish" game.

Great Jewish basketball players, coaches, and executives throughout the years have included Max Zaslofsky, an All-NBA guard in 1947–1950, Eddie Gottlieb, who founded the Philadelphia SPHAS and Philadelphia Warriors, Red Auerbach, who coached the Boston Celtics to 9 NBA titles, Red Holtzman, who coached the New York Knicks to 2 NBA titles, Dolph Schayes, a 12-time NBA All-Star for the Syracuse Nationals, Larry Brown, the current coach of the Philadelphia 76ers who was a star player in the old American Basketball Association (ABA), and David Stern, the current NBA Commissioner.

The Philadelphia SPHAS were one of the most successful professional basketball teams of the pre-NBA era. The SPHAS were organized in 1918 and disbanded in 1949. Originally, it was an amateur team, but it became one of the most dominant teams in the American Basketball League, as it won 7 league championships. All but a few of the SPHAS players were Jewish, and the team uniform had a Jewish Star and Hebrew letters that spelled SPHAS.

Philadelphia's Jewish Basketball League, or JBL, which has operated since 1902, is one of America's oldest leagues. Many outstanding players and coaches got their start in the JBL, including the legendary Temple University coach Harry Litwack, Nat Holman, who played for the Original Celtics, and Eddie Gottlieb.

In the 1920s and 1930s, JBL games drew 1,000 to 1,500 fans, attracted college scouts, and received extensive newspaper coverage. There was genuine enthusiasm in the Jewish community when the JBL was ready to start its season, and women would scream and holler for every basket. Games were played Tuesday and Sunday nights and the Sunday games were followed by a dance. The players would stay around and socialize, and many of them would meet their future wives at the dances. The players may have been enemies on the court, but many became lifelong friends and formed an active alumni association, which currently boasts more than 400 members.

In fact, it's the cultural aspect of the JBL that makes it unique. You won't confuse the JBL's opening game ceremonies with the Chicago Bulls' pre-game light show. At the beginning of each season, Hatikvah, the Israeli national anthem, is played in addition to the Star Spangled Banner. During some seasons, a rabbi says a prayer to protect the players from injury before the opening game of the season, and during Hanukkah, there's a menorah lighting ceremony at half court. Many JBL spectators are alumni who played during the league's glory days of the 1930s.

There are still talented athletes for them to watch, guys who either excelled in high school or leapt to some degree of stardom in college. Sam Jacobs starred for Cornell, earned first-team All-Ivy League honors, and, in 1988, led his team to an Ivy League Championship and the NCAA tournament. Jim Kieserman led his suburban Philadelphia high school to the state quarterfinals in 1988, played significant minutes for the University of Miami Hurricanes basketball team, and won a silver medal as a member of the United States Maccabiah Basketball team in the World Maccabiah Games in Israel.

Other JBL players have played for Temple, George Washington, Princeton, Virginia Commonwealth, Dickinson, and Gettysburg, among other schools.

So if you see Tamir Goodman play for Towson University during his college career, just remember that he's really just part of the ongoing tradition of Jewish basketball.

Article 65
War, Terror Put March Madness in Perspective (Baltimore Sun, reprinted in Charlotte Observer and Deseret Morning News, March 3, 2003)

March Madness, a.k.a. the NCAA men's college basketball tournament, has tipped off, and it's "awesome, bay-bee." Well, this year, it's not quite as awesome. Something is missing.

The outbreak of war in Iraq and the continuing threat of terrorism at home have put things in perspective.

After Sept. 11, many commentators predicted that the tragedy would shift people from focusing on the frivolous. For a while, that seemed to be the case.

Yet our society soon returned its attention to the trivial. Who would win "American Idol"? Whom would "The Bachelor" or "Joe Millionaire" choose to be his mate? As a lifelong, diehard sports fan, I never thought I would conclude that, in the scheme of life, sports and the NCAA tournament are frivolous and trivial. It's only a game. I still like to watch sports, but my emotional investment in the game isn't nearly as high as it was before Sept. 11.

The NCAA tournament is my favorite sporting event. Every March, I go into a cocoon and try to watch nearly every hour of television coverage. I've also seen many tournament NCAA games in person, including the 1992 classic Duke-Kentucky NCAA Regional Final.

As I've done for 10 years, I took off work to watch the first round of this year's NCAA tournament. But I almost felt guilty. Why was I watching No. 14 seed Holy Cross trying to shock and awe No. 3 seed Marquette with a war on?

During timeouts, commercials and halftime of three close games, I clicked over to news coverage. While Marquette's Travis Diener was hoisting up three-pointers, Iraqi oil fields were being set afire, explosions erupted around Baghdad and American ground troops entered Iraq from Kuwait.

While I watch the games, the real world is in the back of my mind. Frequently, I think about the brother of one of my high school soccer teammates who was one of the World Trade Center victims, or about the guy I know from my gym who is fighting in Iraq.

There's nothing inherently wrong at this time of war with losing ourselves in the NCAA tournament as a diversion. The NCAA made the right decision to permit the games go on. There will be many shining moments in the tournament, and new stars will be born.

That said, the past couple of years should have taught us that sports is a diversion. March Madness is fun, but this year I won't be taking it so seriously. After all, only life and death are really life and death.

Article 66
Clarke's Slaps Against Lindros Give Hockey Another Black Eye (Philadelphia Inquirer, April 10, 2000)

Philadelphia Flyers fans will be rooting for the Orange and Black as they battle the Pittsburgh Penguins in the NHL playoffs.

Count me out. Given the way Flyers general manager Bob Clarke has treated star player Eric Lindros during the last few weeks, I'll be actively rooting against the Flyers.

Growing up, when I had most of my hair and Bob Clarke had most of his teeth, I was a huge fan of hockey and the Flyers. I played street hockey almost every day after school. I was sure that Bernie Parent waved directly at me as I marched in the two parades down Broad Street in the mid-70s along with a million other Flyers fans. Black and Orange meant Flyers, not Halloween.

When I grew up, however, my interest in hockey waned. Maybe I outgrew it, much like most adults outgrow the Tooth Fairy, Santa Claus, Pro Wrestling, and the Three Stooges. Over the years, I evolved into a basketball and football fan. The other sports are there, but I really don't care too much about them. It wasn't until last month though that my apathy toward ice hockey turned into hatred.

When Bob Clarke returned as Flyers General Manager in 1994, he hoped to be a mentor to Lindros. Dogged with physical problems in past years, Lindros now is out long-term with a dangerous concussion. Bob Clarke's behavior during the past few weeks has been despicable. He assailed Lindros relentlessly when the latter merely told his side of the story to set the record straight regarding how the Flyers' doctors and trainers had failed to diagnose his grade 2 concussion. At Clarke's behest, the Flyers' players decided to strip Lindros of his captaincy. For weeks, Clarke had indicated that he would require Lindros to apologize to the team, to the team trainer who misdiagnosed him, and to the players for something that should not be the subject of any apology.

Clarke has continued to blast Lindros in every media outlet he can find. The Flyers' players' recent criticism of Lindros reflects their fear of Clarke and indicates that they have as much free speech as a citizen of Cuba or China.

While Eric Lindros hasn't emerged as the next hockey "Messiah" or even the "Mark Messier" that he was supposed to be when the Flyers acquired him in 1992, he has been one of the top players in the league. He has also been a marquee name and has put the Flyers on national television numerous times. He plays an aggressive style of hockey and has given his body up for the team. More importantly, he has been a gentleman and a class act. He doesn't do drugs, hasn't been in jail, and donates a great deal of his time to charitable causes.

Clarke's recent actions are reflective of why pro hockey is a Mickey Mouse, minor league operation in the United States.

The NHL's culture of violence and fighting led to the recent brutal assault by Marty McSorley upon Donald Brashear. In parts of the United States where hockey is not played, the sport is either totally ignored or is considered a joke. Hockey is perceived as WWF Wrestling on ice. It is the only sport in which the referees step away and let the players duke it out like rock-em sock-em robots. Half of the NHL highlights shown on local TV news in places like, say, Charlottesville, Virginia, or Boise, Idaho consist of a fight.

Compared to other major sports, the NHL's Nielsen TV ratings are pathetic. TV ratings for the 1999 Stanley Cup Finals ranged from 2.7 through 3.5. The 2000 NHL All Star Game drew 2.7. Game 5 of the Eastern Conference Final in 1997 between the Flyers and the New York Rangers, two high-profile teams in major TV markets drew a 2.4 rating. In contrast, Game 4 of baseball's World Series in 1999 drew a 17.8, Game 4 of last year's NBA Finals drew a 12.0, and this year's NFL Super Bowl drew a 43.3.

Even minor sports events such as the Kmart Michigan 400 auto race (4.4), WWF Smackdown (5.2), the Buick Invitation Golf Tournament (8.0), and the World Pro Figure Skating Championships (7.4), easily outdraw Stanley Cup Finals ratings.

If and when the Flyers go down in the playoffs, I hope that their loyal lemming fans will have the courage to criticize their beloved "organ-eye-zation." Maybe they can chant Lindros' name, or better yet chant "Blame Bobby Clarke" to the tune of South Park's "Blame Canada."

If the Flyers somehow have a miraculous playoff run and win a Stanley Cup, I hope everyone has a great time at the parade. I'll wait until the Mummers.

Article 67

In This Corner: The Man Who Invented Trash-Talking (Muhammad Ali), Chicago Tribune, December 27, 2001. A revised version of this article was published in the Philadelphia Daily News.

I was never a fan of Muhammad Ali. To a generation of Baby Boomers, Ali may have been a cultural icon and a hero, but to me, Ali was just another successful sports figure to root against, much like Notre Dame, the New York Yankees and the Boston Celtics.

Even though I did the best impersonation of Howard Cosell in my elementary school, I loved it when Joe Frazier knocked Ali down and won their first fight; I seethed inside when Ali outfoxed George Foreman and "shook up the world" in Zaire; I jumped up and down with glee when Ken Norton broke Ali's jaw. When crowds chanted "Ali, Ali, Ali!" I would chant "lose, lose, lose!"

While I admire and respect Ali's tremendous boxing skills and the fact that he spoke his mind and stood for his convictions by sacrificing the prime of his career when he shunned the Vietnam draft on religious grounds, I couldn't stand his trash-talking, self-promotion, showmanship, arrogance and disrespect for his opponents. While he floated like a butterfly and stung like a bee, his words also stung many.

Ali set the stage for everything that many people today don't like about modern-day athletes—dancing in the end zone, taunting fans and opponents, etc. He wrote poetry that predicted in which round he would beat his opponent. Ali referred to himself as "The Greatest," and for years he compared Joe Frazier to an ugly, stupid gorilla and called him an "Uncle Tom." He reportedly mocked Joe Louis for losing his money and for being inarticulate.

I always liked quiet, workmanlike athletes who just did their job on the field, such as Emmitt Smith, Michael Jordan and Joe Frazier, who was the son of a sharecropper and overcame adversity growing up in poverty in South Carolina. When you score a touchdown, just give the football to the referee. When you block an opponent's shot, you don't have to wag a finger in the other player's face.

Berating opponents got so out of hand during the 1990s that the National Collegiate Athletic Association instituted a rule that penalized taunting and celebrating on the field. Even in my experiences playing sports as a kid and as an adult, I always hated the kids who would talk trash and yell stuff like "swing batter, swing batter, he's a whiffer, he's a whiffer." Since I wasn't a Little League All-Star, I took the whiffer comments personally. Even as an adult playing in an over-30 basketball league a few years ago, I seethed inside when someone scored a layup on me and got in my face and yelled, "Take some of that!" There is no denying that Ali was a cultural icon, a humanitarian, and a spokesperson and positive role model for African-Americans. To his credit, he spoke out against racism, had the courage to change his name from Cassius Clay and remained committed to Islam despite public criticism. But he shouldn't be deified in light of his flaws, especially his poor sportsmanship.

So when I shuffle off to see Will Smith portray Muhammad Ali in the upcoming movie, I'll still be rooting for Joe Frazier to land that one extra left hook in the "Thrilla in Manila." Gee, I wish Oliver Stone had been the director.

Article 68
Despite a Snub at the Olympics, He Maintained His Ethnic Pride (Marty Glickman tribute), Philadelphia Inquirer, January 2001.

We all know the stories of Olympic heroes such as Jim Thorpe, Carl Lewis, Rafer Johnson, and Marion Jones—great athletes who took advantage of their opportunity to perform on the world stage and win gold medals.

Marty Glickman never got that chance. Glickman, who died this week at the age of 83, was a member of the United States track team who was removed from the 400-meter relay at the 1936 Berlin Olympic Games. It wasn't a hamstring or food poisoning that kept Glickman from running in that event.

Glickman and another relay teammate, Sam Stoller, were pulled from the race on the eve of the event. United States Olympic team officials told them that because they were Jewish, a victory would embarrass the host Nazis.

Glickman and Stoller were replaced in the relay event by Jesse Owens and Ralph Metcalfe—despite the protests of Owens, who felt that Glickman and Stoller should run. The American 400-meter relay team easily won their race and captured the gold medal.

Glickman went on to have a very successful sports-related career in broadcasting. He announced college basketball games and became the voice of the New York Knicks for 21 years. From 1948 to 1971, he broadcasted games for the National Football League's New York Giants, and he later went on to announce games for the New York Jets. Glickman was inducted into the Basketball Hall of Fame, the Sportscasters Hall of Fame, and the New York Sports Hall of Fame.

Despite his later success in life, Glickman agonized over what could have been and he remained bitter. According to a 1999 article in the San Diego Jewish Press-Heritage, Glickman expressed his feelings to historian Peter Levine about returning to Olympic Stadium in Berlin in 1985 as part of a tribute to Jesse Owens. "As I walked into the stadium, I began to get so angry," Glickman told Levine. "Not about the German Nazis, that was a given. But the anger at Avery

Brundage (Chairman of the United States Olympic Committee) and Dean Cromwell (U.S. Olympic team track coach) for not allowing an eighteen-year-old kid to compete in the Olympic Games just because he was Jewish."

For every story of Olympic glory there are many more stories of those who, like Glickman, were denied the chance to shine on the world's stage.

During the 1930s and 1940s, Eulace Peacock was one of the world's greatest sprinters and long jumpers. While competing for Temple University's track team, he won the AAU 100 meter dash in 1935, defeating a field that included future track Hall of Famers Jesse Owens and Ralph Metcalf. In that same meet, he defeated the future legend Owens in the long jump. Peacock then went on to beat Owens in several other meets that year in the sprints and the long jump. Unfortunately, before the Berlin games, Peacock suffered a pulled thigh muscle that kept him off the 1936 Olympic team. It was Jesse Owens, not Peacock, who went on to become an Olympic and cultural legend. The Olympic Games were canceled in 1940 and 1944 due to World War II, and Peacock was too old to compete by the time the Olympics resumed in 1948.

Michael Brooks was one of the greatest basketball players in the history of the city of Philadelphia. He starred at West Catholic High School and then went on to have an incredible college basketball career at La Salle. Brooks scored 2,628 points during his career, had 51 points in one game, and was named the college basketball player of the year by the National Association of Basketball Coaches in 1980. He was drafted in the first round of the NBA Draft by the Los Angeles Clippers in 1980 with the ninth pick.

Brooks was named captain of the 1980 United States Olympic Basketball Team, which was scheduled to compete in the 1980 summer Olympic Games in Moscow. Unfortunately, the United States chose to boycott those games due to the Soviet Union's involvement in Afghanistan. For all of his great college achievements, Michael Brooks lost his chance to compete on the world's stage.

Eulace Peacock and Michael Brooks and many other potential Olympians were victims of circumstances. Wars, injuries, and boycotts are unfortunate, but they happen. Glickman's story was even more tragic, as it hurt him personally. He and his Jewish teammate were barred from competing in the Olympics simply because of their ethnic origin.

Despite suffering the indignity at the Berlin Games, Glickman didn't lose his pride in his ethnicity. According to the New York Post, Glickman declined to change his obviously Jewish last name so as to enhance his opportunities in the broadcasting business.

The U.S. Olympic Officials may have taken away Marty Glickman's chance at a gold medal, but they couldn't strip him of his Jewish identity.

Article 69

Proposition 48 Closes College Doors To Many Deserving Black Students (Philadelphia Inquirer, January 1994)

The NCAA recently reported that graduation rates of black college athletes had significantly increased. Have proponents of Proposition 48 and its controversial SAT cutoff score of 700 for freshman eligibility been vindicated?

No. The true story behind the numbers shows that many kids, particularly minorities, are being shut out from an opportunity to attend college.

A recently released NCAA survey showed the graduation rate for black male athletes entering school in 1986 increased to 41 percent from a 33 percent average over the period from 1983 to 1985. However, the survey also showed black participation for men and women in Division 1 sports dropped from 27 percent before Prop 48 to 23.5 percent in 1986–1987.

Under Proposition 48, an NCAA bylaw enacted in 1983, incoming freshmen were required to sit out a year and lose a year of eligibility if they failed to achieve a C average in 11 core academic courses or if they failed to score at least 700 on the SAT or 15 on the ACT.

This August, a group of African American basketball coaches decried these NCAA mandates. "It's a crisis because the rule disproportionately hurts blacks and puts hundreds of black kids back on the streets." Drake University basketball coach Rudy Washington, the executive director of the Black Coaches' Association, told me. "Coaches can't change the rule themselves because the public thinks we're only concerned about winning. We're trying to identify and educate black educators who feel our way so as to pressure their peers."

They argue that black athletes—and blacks generally—deserve a better chance to prove they can succeed in college and that SAT scores are not an infallible forecast of future success. In 1993, all blacks seeking college admission averaged 741 on the SAT—only slightly higher than the level required of black athletes—while white students averaged 938.

Students from families with incomes between $10,000 and $20,000—students who are disproportionately minorities—averaged 813 while students from families making over $70,000 averaged 1,005. The relationship between SAT scores and level of parental education shows that the higher the educational level, the higher the mean score.

An example of a school that has moved aggressively to assist disadvantaged applicants—and not simply athletes—is La Salle University. It has an Academic Discovery Program (ADP), which admits about 35 economically disadvantaged students annually. The program's students, primarily minorities, have SAT scores that generally range from 750 to 850, numbers significantly below the average SAT scores for the rest of La Salle's student body. These students receive weekly tutoring and group counseling and participate in an intensive summer workshop before their freshman year.

While ADP students have a lower graduation rate than the rest of the La Salle student body, it is still better than 50 percent—nearly the same as the graduation rate for all college students nationwide. The program has produced many successful professionals.

Many Prop 48 athletes also have succeeded. Take Romaine Haywood, a La Salle University basketball player, who had to sit out last season due to his failure to attain the requisite 700 SAT score. Haywood had a 3.6 grade point average at Atlantic City High School and graduated in the top 10 percent of his class. He is a communications major at La Salle and achieved a 2.8 GPA as a freshman.

"I agree with academic standards, but one test is not a good measure of what someone can do in college," said Haywood. "You have people taking the test coming from different ethnic backgrounds, growing up in different neighborhoods and speaking different languages. Most people think Prop 48 athletes are dumb and lazy, but that's just not true."

Fortunately, Haywood could afford to attend La Salle during his freshman year. Others haven't been as fortunate.

Proposition 48 was enacted in response to horror stories involving athletes who were basically illiterate upon college graduation. The theory was that by enacting the 700 cutoff score, high school athletes would be motivated to study. However, the NCAA chose the wrong approach to remedy a bad situation.

While low SAT scores may reflect lack of motivation, in most cases they indicate that many minority inner-city kids do not have access to an atmosphere that encourages learning. These students endure overcrowded classes, inadequate materials and facilities, and violence. When exposed to intense tutoring and an environment that fosters learning, many inner-city kids, including athletes, adjust to college. SAT scores are merely one factor in determining whether college applicants should be admitted. They should be used as predictive guides, not as an absolute bar to a college education. Each college must be allowed to determine its own guides as to which students to admit.

If urban and black colleges choose to educate a wide range of individuals, including some who do not score well on standardized tests, that should be their prerogative and other schools should not impose their own admission standards. If a college wants to give this chance to athletes who otherwise wouldn't attend school, this again should be determined by each individual school.

The NCAA should focus, instead, on penalizing schools that fail to graduate their players. Why not take away scholarships or limit television appearances for schools that can't graduate 30 percent of their players over, say, a five-year period?

College should be a place where students from all backgrounds have an opportunity to succeed. For black student athletes, Prop 48 makes the playing field uneven and fumbles their chance away.

Article 70
Rubbing Elbows With The Pros. Philadelphia Welcomat (Personal Essay From 1991).

During the summer of 1980, right after my freshman year of college, I worked as a camp counselor at Green Lane, an overnight camp in suburban Philadelphia. A week before the regular camp started, Green Lane hosted a football camp hosted by Ron Jaworski, then the quarterback of the Philadelphia Eagles. We camp counselors were given an option of working at the football camp to perform odd jobs, like selling candy at the canteen. Since I was a fanatical Eagles fan with some time to kill, I took up the offer.

The week turned out to be a sports fantasy come true, as several of the Eagle players came to the camp that week to instruct the kids. Visitors to the camp included Chris Ford, the former Boston Celtic, and Doug Collins, the great former 76ers guard who went on to coach the Chicago Bulls.

My duties at the canteen were minimal. I only had to "work" about two hours a day. That left the rest of the day to watch the football training sessions, play tennis and basketball, and talk to the athletes.

One afternoon, I shot baskets with Harold Carmichael, the Eagles' six-foot-seven wide receiver. Playing one-on-one against Carmichael wasn't really an option, given his nine-inch height advantage. Some of the kids who walked by tried to coerce Big Harold into dunking, but he declined, explaining that the camp sponsors weren't paying him enough. Since they weren't paying me enough either, I too declined.

Many of the Eagles were avid tennis players. Several of them spent almost as much time on the tennis courts as they did teaching the kids. Big Foot Dennis Harrison, at six-foot-eight and 290 pounds, was a menacing sight at the net. However, Max Runager—the Eagles' punter, who was blowing everybody away with his booming serve—was by far the most impressive.

At that time, I was a fairly decent tennis player who had made the La Salle University tennis team as a freshman. I was determined somehow to get to play against Runager before the week was over.

One night, a group of us went to Pepe's, a bar where we knew the players hung out. It was kind of funny seeing a group of pro athletes sprung loose in a bar. They drank kamikazes the way the campers drank Kool Aid. Cliff Stoudt, a back-up quarterback for the Steelers bragged about how the Steelers were going to get "one for the thumb in '81."

The Eagle players responded that maybe the Steelers would win their fifth Super Bowl, but at least they would get some playing time. Since I was under-age, I was nervous for about an hour, hoping that I wouldn't get kicked out of this wild scene. Fortunately, I was one of those 19-year-old kids who looked older than my age; due in part to a well-kept five o'clock shadow that Sylvester Stallone would have been proud of.

After watching Eagles fullback Leroy Harris grunt and shake through his pin-ball game, I figured it was time to find Runager and try to set up a tennis match. I saw him playing a game of darts and waited anxiously until he was finished. After mustering up my courage with the aid of a few beers, I boldly approached Max and introduced myself. He was extremely personable, and we talked for awhile about his career and what was going on at the camp. I told him that I was on my college tennis team and suggested that we hit around sometime. While he surprised me and said he'd like that, I figured he'd forget.

Two days passed and Runager didn't say anything about playing, even though he saw me. I figured he'd forgotten.

However, on the last night of the football camp, upon seeing me, he gave me a big grin and said, "Hey, kid, you wanna play?"

My pulse shot up and I raced to my bunk to get my tennis racket. While I expected to merely hit around, Runager surprised me again by asking if I wanted to play a set.

As we began to play, I sensed that Runager was tired from a long hot day in the sun teaching the kids. His killer serve was off, and my ground strokes were better than usual. Another factor in my favor was that several Eagle players were nearby, standing around a keg of beer watching our match with bated, Budweiser breath and occasionally heckling Runager.

I quickly jumped out to a 4–1 lead, but Max cranked up his Roscoe Tanner serve and rallied to tie the set at 4–4. Visions of blowing my lead and losing the set danced briefly through my head. However, I didn't disappoint our rowdy audience and I took it to the Max; I waltzed through the last two games to take the set, 6–4, thus becoming a camp celebrity for a night.

Runager was a class act in defeat. We talked for a while, and he even invited me to have some beers at the Eagles' keg, an honor bestowed upon few mortals.

Since I felt tired and most of the players had left, I only stayed briefly. Instead, I went back to my bunk, where some of the campers and other counselors chanted, "Larry, Larry, Larry…" I was elated that I'd not only played but beaten a pro athlete in a sport that he was good at. I also felt relieved that I hadn't blown my big lead.

Eleven years have passed since that June week. Runager is retired, my knees are shot, and I've lost all semblances of my ground strokes. But if you're out there Max, I'll be glad to give you a rematch. Don't forget to bring some fans. I'll supply the beer.

Article 71

Leveraging Your Knowledge: Op-Eds and Essays (My Chapter on Op-Eds and essays from The ASJA Guide to Freelance Writing) (St. Martin's Press, 2003).

10,000 pennies for your thoughts?

There are many newspapers and magazines that pay freelance writers to express their opinions in personal essays and Op-Eds. Writers can capitalize on what they know or think by describing their opinions and experiences. Through Op-Eds and essays, writers can share their personal experiences, inspire readers or state a strong opinion that inspires social change. Sometimes it's a way to use what you've learned in your reporting but couldn't use in a news story. It's a way of leveraging what we know or what we think.

Newspapers are the biggest market for essays and Op-Eds, but many magazines also accept opinion pieces or "personal" articles. Most literary magazines run personal essays and programs on National Public Radio often carry commentaries by freelancers; I have done commentaries for "Morning Edition" and "Only a Game," and I know a number of other freelancers who have been on other NPR programs.

While it's flattering to get paid for your opinion, don't quit your day job for this type of writing; it doesn't pay as much as journalism. Most major regional newspapers pay between $75 and $150 for an Op-Ed piece, though some papers occasionally may go as high as $500. Major magazines pay more for personal essays. For instance, Smithsonian pays $1,000 to $1,500 for its backpage humor essays. Most newsmagazines and women's magazines pay comparable rates, but sometimes more or less than that.

Most newspapers encourage Op-Ed submissions of 700 to 800 words. The longest Op-Ed I've written was around 1,000 words, and the shortest was 400 words. Sometimes it's easier to break into a paper with a shorter article. Some papers are very strict about their word length requirements. If a newspaper wants 700 words and you file 1,200, there's a good chance the editor won't even read it.

Length is also important to magazine editors. "When you're writing Op-Eds and essays for magazines, have a specific market in mind," says Stephanie Abarbanel, senior articles editor at Woman's Day. "Notice the length of the articles. You would be surprised how many essays I get that are twice the length that we're looking for."

Despite the seemingly low rates, essays and Op-Eds can be attractive for freelancers since they don't take as much research and reporting as other types of articles. They can also raise your profile both among readers and editors, and they can help you to become established as an expert in your field. If you want to establish yourself as a financial writer, you might want to write Op-Eds when the market is in the news, such as during a boom or bust. If you want to focus on sports, write Op-Eds linked to major sports stories. Doing this type of writing can also help you sell a book by generating publicity, discussions, and controversy.

One advantage of submitting Op-Eds to newspapers as opposed to magazines is that decisions are often made right away. You don't have to wait two months to have someone read your manuscript. In July 2002, I wrote an Op-Ed criticizing the Bush administration's proposed Operation TIPS, which encouraged certain workers to report suspicious information to the government. I researched the article on a Saturday, wrote it on Sunday, submitted it on Monday, and saw it in print in the Chicago Tribune on Tuesday.

SUPPLY AND DEMAND

Competition for the Op-Ed page can be fierce. In Philadelphia, the Inquirer Commentary Page receives approximately 1,200 Op-Ed submissions a week to compete for 10 slots for freelance Op-Eds. On some days, the editor gets up to 600 submissions. However, persistence pays off. For five years I tried breaking into the Baltimore Sun Commentary page. I would send an Op-Ed at least once a month to no avail. However, in 1999, the Commentary Page editor left the paper. The interim editor accepted the first Op-Ed that I sent to her. Then she accepted my next two Op-Eds. She sent an email praising my versatility. When a new permanent editor took over, the friendly interim editor put in a good word for me. I continued to place articles, and occasionally even got assignments to do Op-Eds. Similarly, it took me four years to break into the Chicago Tribune and Newsday, and six years to break into the Atlanta Journal-Constitution.

Sometimes constant rejections might be an indication that you need to work at your craft and improve. As Stephanie Abarbanel of Woman's Day says, "Some writers just aren't ready for a national magazine—the style and content just aren't there yet. But all hope isn't lost; you can work at it and hone your skills. There is one freelance writer who I rejected a number of times during a five-year period. However, she continued to work at it and built up her writing clips by writing for other magazines. This year we published three of her essays."

Timing is critical for newspaper Op-Eds. In 1993, I sent the Inquirer an Op-Ed on the future of Temple University's declining football program from the perspective of a longtime fan. The Inquirer wasn't interested, so I sold the piece to a Philadelphia weekly. The day before it was scheduled to run, I got a call from the Inquirer. The editors had received an article calling for Temple to drop football, and they wanted to run it with my piece, side by side. I called the weekly paper to see if they could cancel my article, but it was too late. The article ran in the weekly. But the story had a happy ending. The following day, Temple's public relations people called and told me that the Inquirer had contacted them to try to generate a positive Temple football article. The public relations department asked me to write another positive Temple article, but with a different slant. A week later, my revised Temple football article ran in the Inquirer.

"Newsworthiness sells," says Philadelphia Inquirer Commentary Page Editor John Timpane. "If you write about timely and hot topics, you will find your way into an editor's heart."

Exclusivity may or may not be an issue. Major national newspapers such as the New York Times, Washington Post and Los Angeles Times require that your submission be exclusive. Most of the national papers have a policy that if you haven't heard from them in two weeks, you're free to assume that it's been rejected and you can submit the article elsewhere. Ann Brenoff, assistant Op-Ed Page editor of the Los Angeles Times, advises, "Do not submit simultaneously to other newspapers. Send to one paper at a time and wait for a response. We ask for five days to consider pieces, but generally respond sooner. I know that when you are writing about something in the news, this may mean you diminish your chances of getting published elsewhere. But we all want to publish material exclusively and violating this rule will mean the major papers won't consider your work in the future."

If you happen to submit articles to a city with more than one major regional newspaper, submit to only one paper at a time. For instance, do not simultaneously submit Op-Eds to the New York Post and the New York Daily News. Most major regional newspapers, such as the Baltimore Sun, Cleveland Plain Dealer, Dallas Morning News and Newsday, allow simultaneous submissions to other regional newspapers in other cities that do not conflict with their circulation areas. To cover yourself, you should inform each publication that you are submitting your article to other major regional papers in other cities, but that your submission to the paper is exclusive to that paper's circulation area. On several occasions, I have sold the same article to several newspapers in different cities. Be aware, however, that you will have to overcome a huge homecourt advantage in many situations. Many, if not most, newspapers prefer Op-Eds by local writers and about local issues. Sometimes it helps to tailor the article to different markets—as I did in selling Op-Eds on youth volunteerism to four different newspapers—Baltimore Sun, Cleveland Plain Dealer, Newsday and Los Angeles Daily News.

"One way to turn off an Op-Ed editor is to send a piece with an introduction that begins, Dear Editor," says Richard Gross, commentary page editor at the Baltimore Sun. "That's an immediate move to the delete button because the editor knows immediately that the piece has been sent everywhere. Newspapers generally like some exclusivity, especially in their own market."

PLACEMENT STRATEGIES

You must decide whether you want to place your article with a national publication such as the New York Times or Washington Post, or whether you want to simultaneously submit your article to many regional newspapers across the country. If you have written an article in anticipation of a major event or holiday, or if you've written an article about a subject that you are confident will drag on for a while (corporate responsibility, church sex abuse, terrorism), you might have the time and luxury of trying to submit to the New York Times for two weeks and then send your article elsewhere if it is rejected.

In 1999, after the Mars Polar Lander crashed on Mars, I wrote an Op-Ed expressing my hope that NASA would dedicate itself to sending humans to Mars by 2015. Then I had to decide where to send my article. If I sent my article to the New York Times, it would have been tied up for two weeks. If the Times had rejected it, the article would have been too stale to send elsewhere. I decided to send my article to many regional newspapers across the country, and it was printed in the Dallas Morning News, Indianapolis Star and elsewhere. In retrospect, it was a good move, because the New York Times ran two Op-Eds on the same subject by space experts.

You don't have to be a doctor, lawyer or Harvard professor to write for the Op-Ed page. Everyone is an expert in something. If you have kids, you're an expert in parenting who can talk about home schooling and corporal punishment. If you're a teacher, you're an expert in education and can write about violence in schools. If you're Jewish, you're an expert on Jewish issues.

In many cases, it is very helpful to set forth personal experiences in your Op-Eds. "We look for people who have a personal connection with the news," says John Timpane. "If you have visited the Middle East on a recent trip or have family members there, that might give you personal standing to talk about it." However, make sure that your personal experience has a connection to the news. "Personal memories that mean nothing to anyone else is a no-no, unless the writer is trying to make a larger point that must be apparent immediately," says Richard Gross.

When Chris Cardone came off the bench to hit two home runs for Toms River, N.J., in the 1998 Little League World Series, I wrote that he had struck a blow for benchwarmers across the country, and I related my experiences as a benchwarmer for my high school soccer team. When my father had difficulty with the Philadelphia paratransit system, some research discovered that it was a citywide problem; I wrote an article based on my father's experiences.

Even when my articles get rejected, I keep them on file in case an issue becomes timely again, or I can rework some of the text into a future article. For instance, during the 1992 presidential election, I attempted to sell an Op-Ed on my distaste for hecklers at political rallies. Unfortunately, there were no takers. I tried again in 1996, to no avail. In 2000, I updated the piece and the Christian Science Monitor accepted it.

Using statistics and getting quotes from experts in the field can also improve your Op-Eds. Anticipate events such as the Super Bowl, a political convention, the start of the baseball season or the start of a new school year. Newspapers like to run Op-Eds with holiday themes such as Mother's Day, Thanksgiving and Valentine's Day.

Unlike newspapers, timeliness is not as essential when it comes to writing for magazines. For one thing, it takes most major magazines at least one month to get a chance to read your essay, and the lead time—from when the story is accepted until it runs—is often three months or more. Therefore, it is helpful to choose a topic or issue that will stay viable for a while. Unlike newspapers, many magazines don't want to consider articles that have been submitted to other publications. Look at Writer's Market or check the magazine's Web site to see whether such submissions are permissible or whether it requires exclusive submissions.

For the most part, there is no need to query when you send a short essay to a magazine; just send the entire text. The editing process can be frustrating for freelancers. Editors for most newspapers make changes on their own without consulting you. They almost always delete text for space and they occasionally will add their own phrases, sentences, or even a paragraph. I think it's reasonable to ask an editor to be consulted about substantive changes or to see the final edited version, but I wouldn't be adamant about it. Many times, editors like to edit their articles the day before they run the story, and it isn't practical for them to get the author's final approval, especially if it's late in the day. It's less of a problem for magazines, since there is less time pressure.

Ideas for Op-Eds are all around you, but you have to be alert. It's as though you're watching a meteor shower in the middle of an empty field. If you turn your head for a second, you might miss one, while someone next to you might see it. Many ideas are sparked by daily interactions with friends and family.

It also helps to have a strong opinion on a certain issue. Don't be wishy-washy. Have something original to say. As Ann Brenoff puts it, "Say something that hasn't been said before. The goal of a Commentary page is to affect outcome, to convince someone to see things your way. Hence we prefer pieces that call for a specific action rather than just comment after the fact on something that has occurred. We are drawn to pieces that have a literary flavor to them, that suggest fresh thinking and new ideas. Stating the obvious won't get you published."

For personal essays, editors like a personal story weaved into a universal subject. The essay must have a point. Unless you extract a bigger truth in your article, you're merely relating an anecdote. The reader should be able to relate to the emotion that you're conveying. Write from the heart and try to make the reader feel that they are not alone. Some personal essay markets for magazines include "Lives" in the New York Times Sunday Magazine, "Back Page" in Smithsonian, "My Turn" in Newsweek, Atlantic Monthly, Hope, Walking, Family Circle, Woman's Day, Conde Nast Bride's, Ladies' Home Journal, Ms., Modern Maturity and Glamour.

"Magazine Op-Eds and essays differ from newspapers, in that newspapers are often more topical," says Stephanie Abarbanel of Woman's Day. "Newspapers and magazines both focus on important issues, but many magazines do it in a more personal way. Our essays at Woman's Day take a more personal perspective. They show that 'I did this' and describe 'My odyssey.' As a national magazine with 20 million readers, our essays have to resonate with a majority of our readers."

Another editor who handles essays, Nancy Clark of Family Circle, looks for 750-word pieces that deal with everyday topics and "make me laugh out loud." Length is 750 words. "To break into the market," she suggests, "writers simply have to write what they know and keep submitting to a broad range of publications until they find one that is compatible with their voice."

There's nothing worse than spending time and effort in researching and writing an Op-Ed and having no one run it. I sell 90 percent of my Op-Eds to at least one publication. If I had a much lower success rate, I probably wouldn't write them as often. Although Op-Ed and essay writing doesn't pay as much as other types of writing, the intangible benefits are enormous. Chances are that your Op-Ed or essay won't change the world, but it might influence local government officials to take action on an issue, make someone laugh hysterically, or cause a reader to change the way he or she perceives life. 10,000 pennies for your thoughts might not seem like much, but if one of your Op-Eds or essays can influence someone or something, the benefits are priceless.

978-0-595-36968-3
0-595-36968-5

www.ingramcontent.com/pod-product-compliance
Lightning Source LLC
Chambersburg PA
CBHW020415290526
45785CB00002B/574